# THE WRIGHT BROTHERS AT KITTY HAWK

## By Donald J. Sobol

Inside illustrations by Wayne Blickenstaff

SCHOLASTIC INC.

New York Toronto London Auckland Sydney

ISBN 0-590-42904-3

36 35 34 33 32 31 30                                    7 8 9/0

Printed in the U.S.A.                                    40

# CONTENTS

1. The Trip to Kitty Hawk . . . . . . . . . . . . . . . . . 7

2. Getting Started . . . . . . . . . . . . . . . . . . . . . . . 15

3. Kite Flying . . . . . . . . . . . . . . . . . . . . . . . . . . 23

4. Kill Devil Hill . . . . . . . . . . . . . . . . . . . . . . . 30

5. At Home in Dayton . . . . . . . . . . . . . . . . . . 38

6. A Great Man Calls . . . . . . . . . . . . . . . . . . . 45

7. Attacked! . . . . . . . . . . . . . . . . . . . . . . . . . . . 52

8. Beyond Kite Flying . . . . . . . . . . . . . . . . . . . 60

9. Wilbur Goes to Chicago . . . . . . . . . . . . . . 67

10. The Magic Box . . . . . . . . . . . . . . . . . . . . . 75

11. Closer to the Goal . . . . . . . . . . . . . . . . . . . 82

12. Almost Perfect . . . . . . . . . . . . . . . . . . . . . . 89

13. A New Kind of Engine . . . . . . . . . . . . . . . 96

14. A Toss of the Coin . . . . . . . . . . . . . . . . . . 104

15. On the Track . . . . . . . . . . . . . . . . . . . . . . . 113

16. Birth of the Space Age . . . . . . . . . . . . . . 120

To Jessie Barckley

CHAPTER 1

# THE TRIP TO KITTY HAWK

WITH STEAM *whooshing* from its sides, the train ground slowly to a stop in Elizabeth City, North Carolina. The car doors opened, and people began getting off. The last off was a young man with many strange boxes.

The station was filled with men and women, waving and calling. They rushed to greet friends and relatives. No one rushed to the young man.

No one knew him. He stood alone, uncertain.

The train pulled out. Soon the station was nearly empty.

"Can I help you?" a workman asked.

The young man answered, "Please — how do I get to Kitty Hawk?"

"Sorry," said the workman, "never heard of the place."

Nobody else around the railroad station seemed to have heard of it, either — a fact explained by the remoteness of the place.

Kitty Hawk was a settlement of hardly two dozen poorly built houses scattered on a narrow strip of land. The strip, connected to the mainland of Virginia, ran southward along the coast for about seventy miles. In North Carolina, it separated Albemarle Sound from the Atlantic Ocean.

The young man walked into town and asked directions of a policeman.

"Kitty Hawk?" said the policeman. "Sure. You take the Roanoke Island Ferry. It makes a trip every week."

"When does it leave?"

"Left yesterday," said the policeman. "If you're in a hurry, hire a boat."

The young man, whose name was Wilbur Wright, returned to the station, moved his boxes to a safe place, and hastened to the water front.

"Excuse me," he said to the first ship's captain he met. "Can you take me to Kitty Hawk?"

The captain shook his head. "Don't know where it is, young fella," he said.

Wilbur had no better luck with the other captains. Some did not know how to get to Kitty Hawk. Others were not interested in making the trip.

Wilbur was not easily discouraged. He took a room in town. For several days he hunted up and down the waterfront. At last he found a captain named Israel Perry, who had once lived in Kitty Hawk.

"It's not much of a place," said Perry. "And it's a forty-mile trip across Albemarle Sound."

"I'll pay you well," said Wilbur. "Where's your ship?"

Perry pointed toward his ship, which lay at anchor. "Isn't she a beauty?"

Wilbur saw a dirty, flat-bottomed old schooner, by no means a beauty. However, he had no choice. Since no other captain would take him, he booked passage with Captain Perry.

An hour later Captain Perry was rowing him and half his boxes toward the schooner in a small boat. Hardly had they left the dock when Wilbur's shoes filled with seawater.

Although he believed the boat was sinking, Wilbur said calmly, "I think you have sprung a bad leak, Captain."

"Oh, we're quite safe," said Perry. "In fact, we're a lot safer than on the big boat."

Perry laughed, though his joke came near the truth. Wilbur found the schooner dirty and full of smells. It was in even worse condition than it had appeared to be from the shore.

Perry seemed at home with the dirt and smells. As both captain and crew, he lived on board the year round. He had faith in the old ship. He sang to himself as he rowed over the rest of the boxes. He lifted anchor and hoisted sail.

The September wind blew strongly. Soon the old ship was moving across Albemarle Sound toward the Atlantic Ocean.

"Not many folks go out to Kitty Hawk this time of year," commented Perry.

"Good," was all Wilbur said.

Perry wondered about his passenger. Finally, he said, "Nothing at Kitty Hawk but a lifesaving station, a government weather bureau, a handful of houses, and a lot of sand."

"And a steady wind, I'm told," said Wilbur. "That's important."

Why was a steady wind important? Captain Perry was more curious than ever about this quiet young man.

"You have friends at Kitty Hawk?" he asked.

"No," said Wilbur.

Perry eyed him thoughtfully. Most of his passengers looked at the water. This young Mr. Wright seemed interested only in the sky. He seemed to be studying the speed of the clouds!

"He's an odd one," thought Perry. "And a mighty calm one, too."

The leak in the rowboat had always scared his other passengers. Often they were so scared they ordered him back to shore. Not this young man.

After a while Perry tried another question.

"Are you in the sand business, Mr. Wright?"

Wilbur smiled. "No, the bicycle business. My brother Orville and I run a shop in Dayton, Ohio."

"I see," said Perry.

But he didn't see at all. Did the boxes hold bicycles? And did this young fellow think he could sell them to people who lived on a sandy strip of land?

Then suddenly Perry had his own problems. All at once the sky grew dark. A storm was upon them. Lightning split the sky. The water rose higher and higher. Waves smashed against the sides of the old ship.

"You're leaking here," called Wilbur. "And here!" No sooner did Wilbur stop one leak than another appeared.

Perry got out two large cans. He handed one to Wilbur.

"Bail!" he shouted.

The two worked hard. As fast as they threw water overboard, more poured in. Icy waves tossed over the sides and leaked in through the bottom.

"We've got to get out of this! Head for the shore!" cried Wilbur.

Water had risen to Wilbur's ankles. His clothes were soaked. With each roll of the boat, he feared his boxes would break loose and dash over the side.

With Perry at the wheel and Wilbur throwing out water, the old schooner swung for the shore.

It was a battle of wood against waves, wind, and rain. The waves crashed, the wind tore at the sails, and the rain drove in with blinding force.

The old schooner tossed and rolled. It groaned like a hurt animal. But it held together. At last it reached the smooth waters of North River. Captain Perry dropped anchor.

"We made it!" shouted Perry. "Did you ever see such a brave old girl?" He patted his ship proudly.

Wilbur shared Perry's joy, though for another reason. None of his boxes had been lost.

When they had cleaned up the deck, the two men went into the cabin to eat. They had worked hard and both were hungry.

Perry ate like a lion, but Wilbur could not touch a thing. The food and the tiny kitchen were as dirty as the rest of the ship.

Wilbur made an excuse and went on deck. In his suit-case was a jar of jelly which his sister Katharine had packed for him. He finished the jelly — the only food he was to have for forty-eight hours!

The weather did not clear until the next afternoon. Captain Perry lifted anchor and sailed from North River. At nine o'clock that night the schooner arrived at Kitty Hawk.

Suddenly Wilbur was excited. He jumped onto the dock and walked inland, but it was too dark for him to see anything.

He stayed on the ship until morning. Then Captain Perry helped him carry the boxes off.

One box, weakened by the storm, broke open as Perry placed it on the dock.

"Say, you sell funny-looking bicycles, Mr. Wright," he said. "Which end are these parts for?"

"They're not for a bicycle," replied Wilbur. "They're for a glider."

Captain Perry scratched his head. "For a *what* — ?"

"For a glider," repeated Wilbur. "For soaring."

"You mean going through the air? Flying?"

"I hope so," said Wilbur.

Captain Perry hurried to his ship, glad he'd already got his money for the passage. This young fellow was crazy!

"If God wanted men to fly, He'd have given them wings," Captain Perry said to himself.

On the shore, Wilbur waved once. Then he turned and walked toward Kitty Hawk, feeling the soft sand beneath his feet and the good strong wind blowing on his face.

CHAPTER **2**

# GETTING STARTED

WILBUR'S BACK still hurt from lying on the deck. His arms were sore from holding onto the boat when it rolled in the storm. He had eaten nothing in forty-eight hours except a little jelly.

But he forgot his hunger and pain. He had reached Kitty Hawk! He breathed the fresh sea air and smiled.

A small boy directed him to the home of William J. Tate. Soon he was knocking on the Tates' front door.

"I'm Wilbur Wright from Ohio," he told the man who opened the door.

"Glad to know you, Wilbur," said the man cheerfully. "I'm Bill Tate, and this is Mrs. Tate. I hope my letter gave you a good picture of the land here."

"It did. That's why I've come," said Wilbur. "The place has everything you said it did."

"Will you try your flying machine tomorrow?" asked Bill Tate.

"No," said Wilbur. He laughed good-naturedly. "It will take at least two weeks to put it together."

Mrs. Tate was less concerned with Wilbur's flying than with his comfort. She learned he had hardly eaten in two days. In a few minutes she laid a large plate of ham and eggs before him.

When Wilbur had finished eating, the Tates showed him their extra bedroom. They told him he must stay with them. They would not take no for an answer.

Early the next morning Wilbur returned to the dock. He got the boxes and set up his tent half a mile from the Tates' house. He broke out his tools and parts and got busy.

Every so often he sat quietly for a moment. Months of dreaming, reading, and planning lay behind him. It was hard, sometimes, not to let his mind race ahead — up into the sky!

Looking out of the tent, he could see Albemarle Sound on his left. The endless Atlantic Ocean lay on his right. The beach itself was five miles long and a mile wide.

"It's just right," he told Bill Tate one afternoon. "Soft sand to fall on. Few houses and no trees to break up the evenness of the wind."

"Plenty of birds to watch, too," added Bill. "Do you study how they fly?"

"I will — later," said Wilbur. "First I've got to travel through the air myself. You can't learn the secret of flight by watching a bird. It's like learning magic by watching a magician. First you have to know what to look for."

Although pleased with Kitty Hawk, Wilbur was not pleased with the way the work went. He had hoped to finish it before Orville, his younger brother, joined him. But after two weeks Orville arrived, and the glider was not yet assembled.

The brothers stayed with the Tates for five days and then moved into the tent. It was large enough to hold them and the glider. Here they could work into the night without keeping the Tates from sleep.

Wilbur had a small gasoline stove. "It'll keep us warm, besides cooking our meals," he said.

Orville agreed to do the cooking if Wilbur washed the dishes.

"That's fair," said Wilbur. "But we can't use the stove yet. The gasoline hasn't arrived."

"You're wrong." It was Bill Tate, standing in the tent's doorway. "The gas is down at the dock now."

"I'll fetch it," said Orville.

"More than gasoline came over on the ferry," said Bill Tate. "I saw five men. They don't live here. I guess they came to see what you're up to."

This news troubled the brothers. They didn't want strangers hanging about, asking questions, getting in the way, slowing up everything.

"I'll tell them to go away," said Bill Tate.

"No, wait," said Wilbur. "We don't have the right. We don't own this land. We'll have to let them take a look and hope they don't stay."

Wilbur wasn't afraid of others stealing his ideas. Indeed, he and Orville believed that no man, no two men, could hope to conquer the air alone. All men who tried to fly had to pool their discoveries.

Still, he did not like strangers around the camp. "When you bring the gasoline," he told Orville, "see if you can learn what those men want."

Bill Tate went with Orville to help carry the gasoline. When they returned, the five men were with them.

"One is a newspaperman," said Orville quietly. "We may have trouble."

"Heard about you at Elizabeth City," said the newspaperman to Wilbur. He stepped closer to the glider. "How big is it?"

Wilbur told him it weighed fifty-two pounds. The

wings had a spread of nearly seventeen and a half feet, with a hundred and sixty-five square feet of lifting surface.

"What did it cost, Mr. Wright?"

"Fifteen dollars," answered Wilbur. A businessman, Wilbur kept careful account of every penny.

The newspaperman began to circle the glider. His eyes grew narrow.

"Don't see where you are going to put the motor," he said suddenly.

Wilbur did not let his anger show in his voice. "It doesn't have a motor," he said.

A sly grin appeared on the lips of the newspaperman. Plainly, he did not believe Wilbur.

"Come on now, Mr. Wright," he said. "Men have been flying for a hundred years. First in balloons. Now in gliders, like this one. I'm onto your secret. Where is the motor?"

"There is no motor," repeated Wilbur.

"You have a big story here. I'm after it," said the newspaperman. "You may be the first person in history to fly a motor-driven, heavier-than-air craft!"

The newspaperman bent low, as if searching for a hiding place in the tent.

"You won't find anything," said Wilbur. "We can't think about using a motor until we know how to glide. Then, if the motor fails, we won't fall like a stone."

"You've got gasoline," pointed out the newspaperman. "If it isn't for a motor, what is it for?"

"For this stove," spoke up Orville.

"A stove burns wood," stated the newspaperman.

"This stove burns gasoline," replied Orville. "Shall I bake you some biscuits? I'm sorry there is no milk, but I'll do my best without it."

"Bake biscuits without milk? On a gasoline stove?" The newspaperman laughed. "This I must see. It will beat flying."

Orville picked up an acetylene lamp that the brothers used for light. He started for the stove.

The newspaperman and his friends jumped back.

"Oh, don't worry," said Orville.

"Are you serious? You'll blow us all to pieces!" cried the newspaperman.

Orville lowered the lamp. The five men believed he really meant to put its flame to the gasoline stove. They turned white.

"This way, gentlemen," called Bill Tate. He held the flap of the tent open. Out raced the five men.

"You can still catch the ferry if you hurry!" Bill Tate shouted after them.

The five men ran across the sand, legs and arms going like crazy.

"I don't think our friends will be back," said Wilbur pleasantly.

"Nor anyone else," said Bill Tate.

He was right. The stunt scared off visitors. During

the rest of the Wrights' stay at camp, no one came again from the mainland. News of the gasoline stove kept even the wood-burning people of nearby Kitty Hawk at a safe distance.

Orville struck a match and carefully lighted the stove. Grinning, he began to bake biscuits.

Bill Tate was the first to taste one. He chewed thoughtfully.

"By golly," he said. "That newspaper fellow was wrong about the stove blowing up. And he was wrong about your not being able to bake good biscuits without milk!"

"He was wrong about something else," said Wilbur.

"What's that?" asked Bill Tate.

"He said other men have flown in gliders like this one," answered Wilbur. "They haven't. No man has tried a glider quite like this one."

Wilbur ran a finger lovingly over the white cloth of the wing. "We've made some changes. We built her with some new ideas."

"If only our ideas are right," said Orville softly.

"We'll know soon," said Wilbur. "Tomorrow we'll take her out and see what she'll do."

CHAPTER **3**

# KITE FLYING

**W**ITH THE FIRST LIGHT of dawn, Bill Tate was back at the Wrights' tent.

"You've got a good wind," he announced.

That was all the brothers needed to hear. They jumped from their cots and threw on their clothes. In their excitement, they forgot to eat breakfast. Helped by Bill Tate, they soon had the glider out on the beach.

Wilbur returned to the tent for ropes. While he was gone, Orville showed Bill Tate how the glider worked. He explained why it was not quite like any other.

"Balance," he began. "That has been the big problem in flight. How to keep the glider riding evenly on the wind."

"Suppose you don't want it to ride evenly," said Bill Tate. "Say you want it to tip. Or to go up. Or to go down."

"That's part of balance too," replied Orville. "Until

now, men have tried to control gliders with their bodies. I mean, by shifting their weight."

"And they failed."

"Not completely," answered Orville. "But controlling a glider with your body is like learning to play the piano with one finger. You might pick out a tune, but you'll never be very good."

Orville pointed to a heavy wire rope running along the double-decker wings.

"This rope controls the side-to-side action," he said. "It does what other men have tried to do by moving their bodies."

Orville placed his hands in the cradle where the pilot was to lie. He gripped the rope and pushed.

"Why, the wings are twisting!" exclaimed Bill Tate.

"We call it *warping*," said Orville. "See the wings on the right side? Their ends are turned upward and forward."

"And the wings on the left side are pulled *downward* and *rearward*," said Bill Tate.

Orville let go of the rope. "Now, in front — "

"Hold on," said Bill Tate. "I'm not sure I understand what I saw."

"The warping is our idea for keeping the glider level," said Orville. Carefully he explained how it changed the way the wind pushed against the wings.

Bill Tate rubbed behind his ear thoughtfully. "I'll have to see what happens in the air," he said. "Maybe then I'll understand. But one thing is clear. You and Will must have done an awful lot of thinking."

"And reading," said Orville. "I guess we've read everything written on flying for the past five years."

Orville walked to the front of the glider. He stopped beside two small wings. They were set about thirty inches ahead of the main wings.

"These small wings are the rudder," he said. He did not go into the principle of a rudder. He merely told Bill Tate what it did.

"It will make the glider go up and down," he explained. "Just as the warping of the large wings makes her tip right or left."

Just then Wilbur returned with rope and string.

In building and planning their glider, the brothers had done everything step by step. Now in testing her, they took the same care. The first step was to fly her as a kite.

Wilbur tied two ropes to the wings. He gave Orville one and kept the other. Next he took strings and tied them to the rudder.

For a moment he gazed in silence at the glider.

"There," he said quietly. "We'll soon know."

"The worst or the best," added Orville. His heart was suddenly pounding.

"All ready?" called Wilbur.

Orville's hand tightened on the rope. "All ready!"

"Then *go!*"

The two brothers ran into the wind, pulling.

The glider moved forward. She seemed to struggle like a wounded bird. She did not rise from the beach.

Something was wrong. The glider should have risen almost at once.

"The wind must have died down," panted Orville.

"Let's try again," said Wilbur. "Pull with all your might, Orv."

Again they ran. Their feet slipped in the soft sand. The wind drove against their chests. The rope bit into their fingers.

Behind them, the glider dragged through the sand, a dead weight.

On they ran, across the white beach. Their legs ached. Their mouths opened wide to catch their breath. In both their minds was one thought: had they made some terrible mistake?

There was a jerk. All at once everything changed. The brothers felt a steady, strong pull against them.

Orville turned around. "She's up!" he sang. "She's up! Look at her, Will!"

A sudden, powerful wind had caught the glider. She soared higher and higher. She climbed twenty feet.

The brothers hung onto the ropes. They fought wildly to keep the glider from carrying them into the sky.

"Don't let go!" shouted Wilbur. "Hold on or she'll end up in the ocean!"

"The rudder," Orville cried. "Bring her lower, Will!"

Wilbur pulled a string tied to the rudder. The glider darted for the ground. Before Wilbur could right her, she had crashed upon the beach.

Because of the soft sand, however, the glider was not wrecked. In an hour the brothers had her as good as new.

"We had better use the derrick," suggested Wilbur. "The wind is getting stronger."

The brothers had built a derrick, just in case they had trouble holding the glider in the sky. The derrick lifted the glider into the air. And it acted as anchor.

Wilbur and Orville were now free to use the control strings. They flew the glider as a kite and were delighted with the results.

By the afternoon, Wilbur was eager for the next step. This was to fly the glider with a man aboard.

Both he and Orville made several trips into the air. They took turns lying flat in the cradle and getting practice with the controls. The derrick kept the machine from soaring away.

By nightfall, the brothers felt greatly encouraged. Of course, further tests would have to be made.

"We'll have to spend a lot more time in the air flying her as a kite," said Wilbur at supper. "We have to be sure our system of balance is right. And we need to gain skill with the controls."

Nature had different plans, however. For days the glider remained in the tent.

Some days the wind blew too strongly. Sand piled against the tent, and the brothers had to dig their way out. After each storm, the people of Kitty Hawk looked out their windows to see if the tent was still standing.

Some days there was no wind at all. Then the brothers found other sport. They fished, and killed fish hawks for food. For amusement they chased chicken hawks along the beach and scared bald eagles. In the evenings, Orville played the mandolin. A friendly mockingbird nearby joined in loudly.

The Wrights had been led to expect winds of fifteen miles an hour almost every day. They soon learned what the figure really meant. Fifteen miles an hour was simply the average for the month!

Because of the winds, neither brother went up in the glider again. Instead, they put on board seventy-five pounds of chains. They worked the controls with strings from the ground.

And all the time they watched how the glider acted. They watched and learned. They made changes and more changes. Still, the glider did not have the lifting power she should.

"Maybe the cloth covering allows some of the wind to get through," said Wilbur. "Maybe the curve of the wings is too small. Maybe everything we've read about the force of air against wing surfaces is wrong."

"Maybe it's our system of balance," said Orville.

"Maybe, maybe, *maybe!*" exclaimed Wilbur. "We've tried the rudder in front, behind, and every other way. I'm so mixed up my head is going around!"

"In another week we'll have to start home," said Orville. "We've spent only one day aboard. What do you say to another maybe?"

"Maybe — what?"

"Maybe we ought to try gliding."

"All right," said Wilbur. He stood a moment, hands on hips, listening to the wind blow angrily across the sands.

"And maybe," he added, "we'll break our necks."

## CHAPTER 4

# KILL DEVIL HILL

IT WAS a huge, ugly hill of sand.

It towered more than a hundred feet into the sky. For unknown years it had stood before the beating of the sea and wind. Men called it "Kill Devil Hill." On its slopes the Wright brothers had decided to try their frail little glider.

Bill Tate came by the tent on the great day. He offered to lend a hand.

Orville thanked him, but refused. "It's our job," he said firmly.

Both brothers felt their friend had done enough for them already.

Wilbur pointed out that Kill Devil Hill lay four miles to the south. "It will be hard going all the way," he said. "There is no reason for you to share the load."

"No reason?" exclaimed Bill Tate. "For weeks I've watched you sail a kite. Do you think I'm going to miss seeing you fly that machine?"

Bill Tate wanted to say more. He wanted to say how much he had grown to like these two quiet, determined young men. But he knew that putting his feelings into words would only make them uncomfortable.

In the end he won out. And the brothers were soon glad for his help. They could hardly have chosen a worse day for the trip.

All nature seemed to rise against them and their strange machine. Sand swept at them, stinging their flesh. Sand caught in their nostrils, ears, and eyes. Sand coated their lips and hair whitely.

But the men were as determined as nature. Slowly they defeated the sand. Nearer and nearer to Kill Devil Hill they dragged their burden of cloth nd wires and ash wood.

Often they had to stop to rest and to wipe sand from their eyes. With their strength recovered, they would start again.

The wind never let up on them. It was an ever-changing fury. It whipped the men and played tricks with the glider.

One instant a gust tried to steal the machine and

toss her into the sky. Then another gust pinned the wings to the ground with the force of a giant.

Few words passed between the three men. They knew what they had to do. And despite the worst that nature threw at them, they covered the four miles. They reached Kill Devil Hill.

Immediately Wilbur climbed to the top. He waved once, quickly.

Orville and Bill Tate read his meaning. The wave said no. No gliding today. The wind was too strong. They had had no experience. Without experience, a test flight in a high wind was both foolish and dangerous.

Wilbur came down the hill, looking tired and beaten. There was a long silence as the three weary men stood beside the glider.

"How long do you think this blow will last?" Wilbur asked finally.

"It might let up tomorrow," answered Bill Tate. "Then again, it might continue for a week."

The brothers could not stay another week. They had

been away from their bicycle business too long already.

"Let's wait one day," said Orville.

"All right," said Wilbur. "But it will have to be tomorrow or never."

For the time being, there was nothing to do. The glider was left at the hill, weighted down with sand. The brothers accepted Bill Tate's invitation to stay at his house.

Hour after hour Wilbur stood by the window.

"The wind won't let up because you're watching," said Orville.

"Not even the birds are out," muttered Wilbur. He shrugged. "You're right, Orv. There's no sense in feeling sorry for ourselves. Let's go to bed."

The brothers fell asleep to the sound of the wind knocking against the house.

Wilbur was the first to awaken. He sat up in bed, listening. The knocking had stopped. Sunshine streamed into the room.

He went quickly to the window. It was a clear,

beautiful morning. The wind was perfect, blowing at about fourteen miles an hour. Nature seemed to say, "I did my worst yesterday. But you wouldn't quit. So here is a day made for gliding. Now let's see what you can do."

They found the glider half-buried by sand. The brothers and Bill Tate spent the morning getting her free. Then they took her up Kill Devil Hill.

Wilbur liked the northeast slope of the hill best. It dropped about one foot in every six.

"You go first, Orv," he said.

Orville was about to argue. The honor of being first belonged to Wilbur, the elder. But Orville knew that argument was useless.

So he lay down in the cradle between the bottom wings. This position put him completely at the mercy of the machine. Other birdmen had sat or stood in their gliders so they could leap free if danger threatened.

By lying flat, the Wright brothers hoped to cut down the wind resistance. They believed the advantage was worth the added danger.

Orville tried not to think of the danger. He took hold of the lever which worked the rudder. He set his feet as if to work the wing warping system.

"All set," he called.

Wilbur and Bill Tate pushed. The glider whispered through the sand. She picked up speed as she moved downhill.

Orville had the feeling of belly-whopping on a sled. The wind whistled past him, smacking his face.

"I'm still not up," he thought. He pulled the rudder to get more lifting power. The glider trembled.

Then he heard Wilbur and Bill Tate shouting. He knew he was off the ground — *flying*.

Suddenly the wings on the right side dipped. They touched the sand. The glider spun around. In an instant she stopped dead. Orville lay in the cradle, breathless but unhurt.

Wilbur and Bill Tate rushed over, making the sand shoot behind them.

Orville got to his knees. "How high was I?"

"Two feet at least!" cried Wilbur. "Are you hurt? How did the rudder work?"

Questions came thick and fast. Orville answered all but one: *"How did it feel to fly?"*

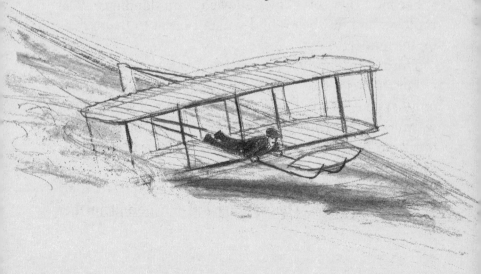

He had never felt anything like that glide. He could not put his feelings into words.

The flight had lasted less than eight seconds. The machine had risen barely two feet off the ground. But that morning of October 17, 1900, was one neither Wilbur nor Orville ever forgot. A dream was coming true.

Wilbur took over and made a glide. Then it was Orville's turn again. In all, the brothers made twelve glides, rising as high as three feet, at speeds up to fifteen miles an hour. Each glide lasted between five and ten seconds.

Along with the fun, the Wrights had learned three important things.

First, their machine picked up speed while keeping the same distance above the side of the hill. This meant she could glide on a slope that need not be so steep.

Second, the soft sand allowed safe landings. The brothers had hit the ground without harm to themselves or the glider.

Third, the controls seemed to work as expected.

For the first eight glides, the brothers used the rudder only. When they felt at ease with it, they loosened the warping wires. During the last four glides they worked the front-to-back balance and the side-to-side balance at the same time.

With the twelve glides, the brothers completed their flying for the year. The weather did not permit further tests.

They left the glider at Kill Devil Hill and broke camp. They were happy with the machine and unhappy with themselves.

They had hoped to gain hours of experience in the air. Instead, they had flown aboard the "kite" for a mere ten minutes. The total time spent in free flight, or gliding, was but two minutes!

On the way down to the dock they stopped to bid good-bye to Bill Tate.

"If everything goes well," said Wilbur, "we'll be back next year."

"I'll be looking forward to it," said Bill Tate as he shook hands. "What about the machine? Don't you want her any more?"

"No," replied Orville. "Next year we'll have a bigger machine. One that will fly farther."

"If you're through with her, may I have her?" asked Bill Tate.

Mrs. Tate made good use of the French sateen cloth which covered the wings. She cut out and sewed dresses for her two daughters. It was better material than she could buy in the stores.

A week after Wilbur and Orville had departed, a neighbor of the Tates admired the dresses.

"What a pity," the neighbor said, "to waste such fine cloth on a kite!"

## CHAPTER 5

# AT HOME IN DAYTON

IT WAS GOOD to be back in Dayton. Kitty Hawk had been exciting and fun. But the small frame house at 7 Hawthorne Street was home.

None of the family was there when the brothers arrived. Carrie Kayler, the hired girl, met them at the door.

She was fourteen, and no bigger than a minute. Orville greeted her with a twinkle in his eyes.

"How long have you been with us, Carrie?" he asked.

"You know very well, Mr. Orville. Nine months."

"And how much have you grown in that time?"

"I'll show you!" said Carrie with a toss of her head.

She marched into the kitchen. Beneath the gaslight she stopped and stood on tiptoe.

"There," she said, turning on the light. "I can reach it without a chair now!"

Orville stroked his chin thoughtfully. "It appears that you might be of some account after all," he teased. "What do you think, Will?"

"If she grows another half inch, we ought to let her stay on," said Wilbur, grinning.

"I'll grow. Wait and see!" said Carrie, who was not only to grow but to stay on as part of the Wright household for nearly fifty years.

Wilbur and Orville were tired after their long trip. By the time they had washed and changed their clothes, it was near dinnertime. Wilbur made hungrily for the kitchen.

The brothers' taste in food, as in everything else, was simple. Wilbur's one weakness was gravy. It had to be smooth. He hated lumps.

As he reached the bottom of the stairs, the front door opened. In walked his sister, Katharine, and their father, Milton Wright. Katharine, the youngest in the family, threw her arms around her brother.

"Will!" she cried joyfully. "You're back — safe!"

"Of course," he said, kissing her. "We promised you we wouldn't hurt ourselves."

She felt his arms and back, searching for broken bones. She looked him over as she might one of her pupils who had played hooky from school. "You've lost weight. We'll have to fatten you up."

Orville heard the voices and hurried down. He and Wilbur had to tell all about their adventures at Kitty Hawk. The talk carried them from the entrance hall to the living room and then to the dinner table.

There were only four of them around the table. Mrs. Wright had died while the children were still small. The two oldest sons, Reuchlin and Lorin, had married and moved away.

"Let us bow our heads and pray," said Mr. Wright, a bishop in the Church of the United Brethren in Christ. Humbly, he offered thanks for Wilbur's and Orville's safe return. Then little Carrie came in with the food, and the talk of Kill Devil Hill, sandstorms, and high winds flowed again.

Mr. Wright listened respectfully. He had a turn for mechanics himself, having once invented a typewriter. He had not, however, got past the idea stage.

How much better his sons had done! From their idea they had built a full-sized glider. And they had traveled four hundred miles to test it.

"We ran into one problem that puzzled us," Wilbur was saying. "According to everything we've read, the machine should have had greater lifting power than —"

He stopped suddenly. He ran his fork through the gravy on his plate. He tasted it and frowned.

"Excuse me," he said. Picking up the gravy bowl, he went into the kitchen.

"Here, Carrie," he said cheerfully. "I'll pour this out,

and we can start over."

Rolling up his sleeves, he got out a pan and set to the task. As Carrie watched, he made the smoothest gravy she had even seen.

Back at the table, Wilbur completed his sentence.

"It did," he said, as if everyone could follow him quite easily.

Wilbur did not usually jump up during a meal. But the desire to have things done right was an old habit. Moreover, the problems of tomorrow always had to wait till the problems of today were met.

Once settled at home, the brothers wasted no time in getting down to business — repairing, manufacturing, and selling bicycles.

The bicycle shop served them well. It gave them a living. More important, it trained them as mechanics. They were able to build with their own hands what they thought up. Other men interested in flying had to hire workmen to carry out their plans.

"Hired men pay no attention to anything but the thing they are told to do," Wilbur said. "They are blind to everything else."

Poor workmanship, the brothers knew, was the greatest danger to a flying machine. They vowed always to do the building and repairing themselves.

By working on the new glider at night, they hoped to have it ready before the busy season. From March to June the bicycle trade was at its height. If they finished the flying machine before then, they could start for Kitty Hawk early in July, instead of September.

"That will give us more time to practice," said Wilbur.

The new glider was to be constructed on the same design as the old one, but with some changes.

The old glider, they believed, had failed to lift well because it was too small. Therefore, they decided to lengthen the wingspread from 17½ feet to 22 feet.

"That will give her a lifting area of 290 square feet. as against 165 square feet on the old machine," said Wilbur.

"And she'll weigh twice as much; nearly a hundred pounds," said Orville.

"She'll be big," agreed Wilbur. "Bigger than anyone has ever tried to fly."

"You mean *dared* to fly," said Orville.

The two brothers stiffened. The thin flame of the gaslight flickered over them as they stood in the bicycle shop. For a long moment neither spoke. The same thoughts ran in both heads.

They might spend all their money building machines that never would completely succeed. They might follow their interest in the sport to one end: their deaths.

"Let's not think about that," said Orville quietly.

Wilbur nodded. He picked up a pencil and continued with his figuring.

"Suppose we increase the curve of the wings to the shape on which Lilienthal based his tables of air pressure," he said.

"Then to hold her up in the wind of seventeen miles an hour, we'll have to keep the wings at an angle of five degrees," said Orville.

"No, I think less," said Wilbur. "Three or four degrees is more like it."

They argued the point. It went like that, night after night — arguing, figuring, working. Sometimes Wilbur would end up agreeing with Orville, only to find Orville had come around to *his* point of view.

Steadily they were getting the job done. They did it in their bicycle shop, working with their hands, reading what other men had accomplished, and remembering how their first glider had acted.

They also got help from Octave Chanute.

Chanute was a famous railroad engineer. Besides, he was the most learned man on the history of flying, and a friend to anyone concerned with the subject.

Wilbur had written to Chanute when he was first bitten by the urge to fly. After his return from Kitty Hawk, he had written again.

"My brother and myself spent a vacation of several weeks at Kitty Hawk, North Carolina, experimenting with a soaring machine," Wilbur had begun. Then he went on to tell of the results.

Not long afterward, Katharine brought Wilbur a letter. She saw his face light up.

"It's from Mr. Chanute . . . Orv, listen to this!" he called across the shop.

Wilbur's eyes raced down the page. "He wants to write up our flights in *Cassier's Magazine* . . . he'd like to know how our names should appear: 'W. Wright & Brother' or 'Wright Brothers.' "

Orville snatched the letter and read it himself. The brothers fairly danced around the shop. The famous Octave Chanute asking for the right to mention them in a magazine!

When they had recovered, they decided it was unwise to give out a full report of their flights. Too much was still unknown.

They wrote Mr. Chanute, explaining their feelings in the matter. If he cared simply to mention that they had made several glides, that would be fine. Wilbur thought "Messrs. Wilbur and Orville Wright" was a good title for them.

Finally they invited Chanute to visit them and to see the new glider they were building.

Chanute wrote back that he would visit them in June. His letter filled the Wrights with a sudden and terrible doubt.

Suppose the great man traveled all the way to Dayton only to find their glider was not worth the long trip?

CHAPTER **6**

# A GREAT MAN CALLS

LITTLE CARRIE KAYLER rushed from the window. "Miss Katharine! Miss Katharine! They're coming up on the porch!"

Katharine Wright cast a last look at her luncheon table. She wanted everything to be just right for Mr. Chanute. Nervously, she smoothed her dress, took a deep breath, and opened the door.

A heavy man of seventy with a white beard stood between her brothers.

Katharine smiled her welcome, and shot Wilbur a

questioning glance. He gave her a quick grin.

The grin said, "He's a regular fellow. He won't throw a fit if your dinner isn't perfect."

Octave Chanute bowed. "Good morning, Miss Wright," he said gently. "Wilbur and Orville have been telling me about you on the way from the station. You are quite as pretty as they promised."

"See?" whispered Wilbur as he passed into the house. "Nothing to be afraid of."

But Katharine was afraid — afraid for her two brothers. This white-haired man built bridges and railroads. He wrote books. He counted as his friends the rich and famous people of the world.

Could her two brothers, who had not gone beyond high school, hold their own with such a man?

Katharine felt she must help Will and Orv. After all, she had gone to Oberlin, one of the very best colleges in the country.

She had planned things to talk about. Without her brothers knowing it, she had read everything she could find about Octave Chanute. She hoped to keep the conversation lively and interesting.

Long before their guest sat down at the table, Katharine found herself unneeded. The men had soared off into the clouds. The talk left her far behind.

As the morning wore on, she noticed a surprising thing. Mr. Chanute talked less and less. He listened more and more.

Katharine grew prouder and prouder. She no longer was afraid. Her brothers could hold their own.

At the table, Chanute, Wilbur, and Orville discussed the failure of great men to conquer flight.

They talked of Leonardo da Vinci, the artist who could do almost anything; of Sir Hiram Maxim, the inventor of the automatic gun; of Charles Parsons, the inventor of the steam turbine; of Dr. Alexander Bell, the inventor of the telephone; of Thomas Edison, the inventor of the phonograph and the electric light.

"All of them have tried to fly — all have given up," said Chanute sadly. He looked at Wilbur. "They spent too much time in figuring and too little in doing. Is that your belief?"

"It is," said Wilbur. "Figuring is necessary, but you must get into the air, too."

"There are two ways to learn to ride a horse," said Orville. "One is to get into the saddle. The other is to sit on a fence and watch, and then go into the house and figure out the best way to overcome the jumps and kicks. Sitting on the fence is safer. But sitting on the horse turns out more good riders."

"Surely you approve of Professor Langley's work, and of Sir Hiram's?" asked Chanute.

Wilbur did not approve at all. But Samuel Langley was head of the nation's Smithsonian Institute in Washington, D. C., and Sir Hiram Maxim was a famous inventor.

So he answered carefully. "Professor Langley is still building models. Trying bigger and bigger ones. And now, I've read, one with a motor. Some day he expects to build a machine large enough to carry him into the air."

"As for Sir Hiram," continued Wilbur, "he started at the other end. With very little real knowledge, he keeps building full-sized machines. I don't believe either Langley or Sir Hiram is going at the problem properly."

"Then what of Otto Lilienthal, the German?" asked Chanute. He spoke like a man who had baited a trap and now was closing in. "Lilienthal, before he was killed, made over two thousand glides in five years. Altogether, he had five hours in the air. If practice is the key, he should have unlocked the mystery of flight."

"Five hours in five years! Could you learn to ride a bicycle like that?" demanded Wilbur. "Hundreds of lessons lasting only ten seconds each? No, you couldn't. And you can't learn to fly that way, either."

Orville feared Will was getting a little hot under the collar. Their guest might become angered. So he said lightly, "We have a name for our system. We call it 'flying by the seat of your pants.'"

Octave Chanute's lips parted in a hearty laugh. "That's a good one," he said. "That's the best way, after all."

The best way, yes. But the older man knew that the seat-of-your-pants system required two things. One was courage, which these two young men obviously had, though they did not speak of it. The other was great sums of money, which they obviously did not have.

Chanute wondered how these brothers would receive an offer of money to further their work. Although he might insult them, he was determined to make the offer.

"The United States is very interested in producing a flying machine," he began. "Did you know the Government has given Professor Langley thousands of dollars to carry on his tests?"

"We read that in the newspapers," said Wilbur.

"It will take a lot of money before a true flying machine is developed," said Chanute.

"We have enough," said Orville. "Our first glider cost fifteen dollars. Our second will not cost beyond our means."

"The further you go, the more costly it will become," Chanute warned. "I have many rich friends. I am sure some of them will be happy to back you in your work."

"No," said Wilbur firmly. "We will bear the costs ourselves."

Chanute sighed. He admired these brothers for refusing his offer. Yet he was puzzled. "Don't you want to make money?" he asked.

"We certainly do," answered Wilbur frankly. "We are businessmen."

"We hope to make a fortune someday — manufacturing bicycles," said Orville.

"To regard flying as a means of earning a living is

foolish," said Wilbur. "No one will ever make any money from it."

"As you wish," said Chanute, giving up. "Now where is the new glider?"

The brothers took their guests to their bicycle shop, a former dwelling on West Third Street.

"As you can see, we do our own repair work as well as selling new and used machines," said Orville.

"Over there are the bicycles of other manufacturers," said Wilbur. "Here are our own makes, the Van Cleve, the St. Clair, and the Wright Special."

Chanute praised the Wright Special as the best buy he had seen. It sold for only eighteen dollars. "Did you always want to make bicycles?" he inquired.

"We always liked to build things," replied Orville. "When Will was a small boy, he had a job folding the weekly church paper. He invented a machine for doing it faster than by hand."

"And Orv invented a calculator that could add and multiply," said Wilbur as he led Chanute to the drawings of the new glider.

Immediately the talk returned to flying and Kitty Hawk. Chanute was shocked to learn that the brothers had not had a doctor at their camp and that they did not intend to have one.

Chanute said he knew a young man, George Spratt of Pennsylvania, who was interested in soaring, and who had had some medical training. Would the Wrights have him at their camp?

Because it was Chanute who had asked, the brothers agreed. They also agreed to have E. C. Huffaker of Tennessee, who was building a glider for Chanute.

As he took his leave, Chanute promised, "I'll stop at Kitty Hawk myself, if it's at all possible."

On the train, the famous engineer thought of his promise with a smile. "If it's at all possible." It would be impossible to keep him away!

For these self-taught Wright brothers had changed his entire thinking. He had always held that success in flying must come from a *group* of men, working together.

And now in Dayton, Ohio, he had suddenly found the group he had said was needed — inventors, engineers, mathematicians, mechanics, and merchants.

All in two young bicycle makers, Wilbur and Orville Wright.

## CHAPTER 7

# ATTACKED!

THE BROTHERS barely recognized Kitty Hawk in July, 1901.

Many of the trees at the edge of the beach were down. Sand was piled high against the houses. The roof of one house was torn off.

"Had a little storm," said Bill Tate. "It blew over yesterday, but I'm still picking sand out of my eyebrows."

"As long as Kill Devil Hill is still standing," said Orville, "we won't complain."

"It's about the only thing in these parts that didn't get moved about a bit," said Bill Tate. "The anemometer

cups at the weather station broke when the wind reached eighty-three miles an hour."

Wilbur looked at the sky. Fat gray clouds were gathering. Suppose another storm struck in a few days and wrecked the glider? What then for the work and dreams of a year?

"The winds have passed," said Bill Tate. "Likely, though, we'll have more rain. It's been dry here for seven weeks."

The brothers stayed that night with the Tates. In the morning, they started for Kill Devil Hill to set up camp.

The rains found them there. By the time the last tent peg was pounded in, the brothers were soaked.

And thirsty. By camping at Kill Devil Hill, they were near their practice grounds, but a mile from drinking water. One trip through the rain decided them: they would sink their own well.

It proved to be a long, hard job. On the very first attempt, the point of their pump came loose and was lost in the sand. For two days they met failure. As with everything, they stuck at the job. Finally, Wilbur drove a piece of pipe twelve feet deep and hit water.

The next day being Sunday, the brothers did no work. But the first thing Monday they started on the shed for the new glider, which was too big to keep in the tent with them.

Despite rain, they had the building up in three days. Built of wood lined with tar paper, it stood 25 feet long, 16 feet wide, and 7 feet high. The wall at either end was a door, allowing the glider to be moved in and out easily.

The camp now had a permanent look. It told the world that neither wind nor rain, cold nor heat, could chase these brothers away. They had come to stay. This tiny spot on the great open beach belonged to flying.

It also belonged to the mosquitoes.

When Octave Chanute's friends, E. C. Huffaker and George Spratt, arrived, the rain had stopped. But a black cloud of insects buzzed across the sky.

Soon everything was covered with mosquitoes. They chewed through socks and shirts and underwear. There was no escaping, no place to hide.

Normally, insects swarmed to Kitty Hawk in the summer. Not even the oldest inhabitant, however, could recall anything like this, a full-scale mosquito invasion.

"The rain must have brought them," Spratt said.

"Never mind how they got here," said Wilbur. "How do we get rid of them?"

"I'd sure like to know!" exclaimed Huffaker. "I've got lumps as big as hen's eggs."

Buzzing, buzzing, buzzing. Tiny black dots flew in and out of the building. The men danced about, beating their arms and slapping their faces and necks.

"It's a losing battle, boys," said Wilbur. "We can't escape them. We've got to outthink them."

"Right," agreed Orville. "After all, we have the brains."

"I'd rather have a thick skin," said Huffaker.

"Then put one on," said Wilbur.

"How?"

"In bed."

"That sounds reasonable," said Huffaker.

Although it was only five o'clock, the men wrapped themselves tightly in their blankets.

"Keep covered," warned Wilbur. "Don't give them a target."

"I've just got my nose out to breathe," said Huffaker. "Five of the little villains are buzzing around it now."

Presently the buzzing faded away, and Huffaker called, "They've given up."

"No question about it," said Wilbur. "We outsmarted them."

He had spoken too soon. For suddenly the cool breeze died down. The air hung heavy and hot. The men steamed in their blankets.

They tried taking off part of their covers. Each time they did, the mosquitoes attacked anew. The hours passed in suffering and slapping, without sleep.

The morning brought relief. The men rose, counted their wounds, and looked for the enemy. The air was clear.

"Maybe they all went for a swim and drowned," suggested Spratt.

"They'll be back tonight," said Wilbur. "Meanwhile we can finish putting the glider together."

The mosquitoes hadn't drowned. They seemed just to have waited for the men to settle to their tasks. Then they swarmed.

"Abandon ship!" hollered Wilbur, jumping up.

Orville, Spratt, and Huffaker were already on their feet and running. The glider was left in the shed with the all-conquering mosquitoes.

"We're men, and they are only insects," said Wilbur.

"Oh, you give me new spirit, you do," said Orville,

rubbing his bites. "What have you in mind?"

"We'll throw up a defense," said Wilbur. "Let them beat themselves silly against it!"

By evening, the men had raised frames and mosquito nets over their cots. They set the cots thirty feet from the shed. Into their net castles they crawled. They lay back, smiling, awaiting the charge of the enemy.

Before long a faint buzzing sounded.

"Here they come!" shouted Huffaker, whose cot stood farthest out.

The buzzing grew louder. Orville saw a mosquito light on the net above him. Then another. Soon the entire top of the net became a moving, living black sheet.

"Report from the southwest," he called. "Enemy hardly has standing room left."

"Mine are already sitting piggyback," said Wilbur.

"Let them sit," said Orville. "Let them sit till they die from hunger."

"Let them eat their hearts out," said Spratt.

These words were hardly spoken when a loud slap and a louder cry were heard.

"Who was that?" Wilbur shouted anxiously.

"Me!" roared Huffaker. "They're getting through."

At that instant Wilbur himself felt a bite. The mosquitoes poured in upon all four men at almost the same moment.

It was a hand-to-hand battle, fierce and short. The men were outnumbered. The castles fell. Spratt and Huffaker fled across the sand. Wilbur and Orville followed seconds later. Two hundred feet away they found safety.

"It can't be any worse," panted Wilbur.

"Anyway, we always have a choice," Orville said. "We can leave camp, or we can be eaten alive attempting to save it."

"I won't give up," growled Wilbur. "I'll stick to my guns. . . . Guns?" He snapped his fingers. "Of course! Guns . . . fire power, that's what we need."

"I never shot a mosquito," said Huffaker. "But I'd be very happy to try."

The "fire power" Wilbur had in mind had nothing to do with guns, however. The next day the weary men searched the beach. They carried back to camp stumps of trees, old boxes, driftwood — anything that would burn. They piled it all around the camp.

Wilbur set fire to the piles of wood. A towering circle of smoke rose skyward.

"It's working," said Orville, after an hour. "I haven't been bitten yet."

"They'll never find us," said Wilbur. "I told you. They're just mosquitoes. No match for brains."

Perhaps the smoke had fooled the mosquitoes. Perhaps they had simply tired of feeding on the same four humans. At any rate, the men lay down that night with no buzzing over them, but plenty of smoke.

Spratt declared the smoke was worse than the mosquitoes. He took his blanket and walked, choking, out onto the beach. A few minutes later he hurried back.

"I was wrong," he said. "The mosquitoes are worse."

The others did not hear him. After being awake two nights, they were sound asleep.

In the morning both mosquitoes and smoke had disappeared.

"A perfect day for the beach," said Orville.

"For looking at it," said Wilbur. He pointed to Kill Devil Hill. "From up there."

With the mosquitoes gone and the fires burned out, there was nothing to delay the test of the big new glider.

CHAPTER **8**

# BEYOND KITE FLYING

IT WAS A FINE DAY for gliding. There was only one trouble: the wind. It blew at only thirteen miles an hour. The new machine was designed to fly in a wind of eighteen miles an hour or more.

Wilbur and Orville believed the slope of Kill Devil Hill would make up for the lack of wind. Spratt and Huffaker worried over the danger.

"We should try her as a kite first," said Huffaker. "If anything goes wrong, no one will be hurt."

"I've had enough of waiting," said Wilbur. "We've been

here more than two weeks and we haven't been in the air yet."

"Hold off one more day," Huffaker begged. "The wind is bound to pick up."

"We might not have the proper wind for another two weeks," said Orville. "Last year we delayed too long. We got in only one day of free flight."

"Then fly her as a kite this morning," said Huffaker. "If she acts all right, take her up the hill this afternoon."

"Are you afraid she'll fall apart?" asked Wilbur with a smile.

"You know better," said Huffaker.

"Yes, I do," replied Wilbur. "I was only joking. How do you stand, George?"

George Spratt nodded at Huffaker. "I agree with Huff. It doesn't make sense to risk your life. Find out first if the machine is safe."

"The machine is safe," said Wilbur firmly. "As for the risk"—He shrugged. There would always be the shadow of death in the air.

He turned to his brother. "What's your vote, Orv?" he asked. "Kite or hill?"

"One vote for the hill," said Orville.

"That's two votes," said Wilbur. "George?"

Spratt kicked the sand. "I've spoken all I'm going to. No matter what I say, you fellows are going to glide. So make it three votes for the hill."

"And you, Huff?"

Huffaker looked at Wilbur, then at Orville. "I've been working too long for model builders," he said slowly. "Can't get used to men who believe you learn to fly by flying."

He shook his head in wonder. "All right, four votes for the hill."

Quickly the glider was carried from the shed. The trip up Kill Devil Hill was slow, hard work.

"You'll get used to it," said Orville to the two helpers. "The first hundred trips are the hardest."

"I hope they get harder and harder," Spratt answered. He pointed to a spot a mile away. "Reach there, and I'll carry her back myself!"

"I'll settle for three hundred feet," said Orville.

To get the feel of the new machine, each brother made three short glides.

"She feels heavy," said Wilbur.

"That may be due to the wind," said Orville. "Or the fact that we aren't giving her a full chance."

"Then I'll give her a chance," said Wilbur.

He lay down at the controls again. Now there would be no attempt to hold back the big machine.

Orville, Spratt, and Huffaker stood by the wings. At Wilbur's command, "Go!" they pushed as a team. The big glider moved down the hill. Suddenly she was off the ground, soaring free. She seemed to float in the air for minutes.

She hit the sand, bounced, and slid gently to a halt.

Orville checked his stopwatch. He knew without looking that it had been a good flight.

"Nineteen seconds!" he shouted to Wilbur.

Despite the poor wind, the glide had lasted longer than any the year before.

Huffaker and Spratt were amazed. They ran to measure the distance. It was three hundred and fifteen feet.

Huffaker threw up his arms. "The longest glide ever!" he cried.

Wilbur thought three or four other men had made longer glides. Still, for the first real attempt, the distance was encouraging.

A dozen flights followed. The results were sometimes good, sometimes disappointing. Then a strange thing happened.

Wilbur was doing the gliding. The machine rose higher and higher. At a height of about twenty-five feet, she came to an almost dead stop. Then she dropped flat upon the sand.

Wilbur climbed out, unhurt. He brushed sand from his clothes. He looked very serious.

He said, "That's the same fix Otto Lilienthal, the German birdman, got into when he was killed. His machine fell headfirst to the ground."

"Do you know why she acted like that?" asked Orville. "I thought her front went up. Did you feel it?"

"I'm not sure. We might have run into a gust of wind," said Wilbur. "I'm just not sure."

"Anyway, the machine is safe against that kind of trouble," pointed out Huffaker. "She wasn't scratched."

"You ought to be satisfied with this day's tests," said Spratt. "She didn't fail you as Lilienthal's machine did him."

"Thank God for that," said Wilbur softly.

The glider had proved safe — and hard to control. After a few more glides, the brothers called it a day.

During the next week they tested the machine as a glider and a kite. Wilbur kept a diary. His notes were different for each day. Those for July 30 were:

### Kite Test
Area 290. Weight 100.
Speed of wind 17 miles. 7.58 meters indicated
   per sec.
Angle 10°. Total pull 18 lbs.
Curvature 1/17.
Estimate head resistance 6 lbs.
Ratio of lift to drift at $10 = 100 \div 12$.

On August 5th Octave Chanute visited the camp, as he had promised. By then the brothers had made more than a hundred glides. And the machine had undergone many changes.

"She doesn't handle as well as the one last year," reported Wilbur. "We don't think the trouble has anything to do with size, though."

"The smaller machine had less curve in the wings," said Orville. "It may be that the large curve fights the wind."

"What about your system of balance?" asked Chanute.

"The warping works fine," answered Orville. "Except that about one time in fifty it doesn't work at all."

"And for no good reason," put in Wilbur.

"As for the old problem of lift, it's as bad as ever. It has about one third the lifting power we figured it would have," said Orville.

Chanute wished to see for himself. He stayed to witness six days of testing. He too was puzzled by the failure of the glider to lift well.

"The trouble isn't with the machine," said the older man. "It is built beautifully. There can be but one way to explain the mystery. The tables of air pressure we are using — you, I, everyone — are wrong."

Chanute had voiced the brothers' own fears. Long ago they had begun to doubt the tables. The great German birdman, Otto Lilienthal, had written the tables. So the Wright brothers had assumed they were correct.

"We based all our work on Lilienthal's tables," said Wilbur, half to himself. He felt as though the ground had suddenly dropped away.

"Don't let yourselves become discouraged," said Chanute kindly. "You have already gone farther than anyone else in the world."

Again and again the older man told the brothers they were making great headway. He knew they were downhearted and might quit.

After he returned to Chicago, the brothers succeeded with their two longest glides: 366 feet and 389 feet.

But these two flights helped their spirits only a little. They were not out to break records. They were out to gain control of their machine. And the machine still did not lift as they had expected.

Then even the weather turned against them. Rain fell for days. The wind blew from the south, the wrong direction. Everything seemed to go bad at once.

At daybreak on August 22 they left Kitty Hawk. Both felt it was a waste of time to go on. They had failed.

Bill Tate saw them off. "See you next year," he called as their boat pulled away.

The brothers merely waved. They did not plan to return to Kitty Hawk.

To continue with flying meant starting all over. Almost nothing done by other men was of any use to them. Instead of picking up where others had left off, they would have to go back to the very beginning.

A new set of air-pressure tables was needed. For that huge task they didn't have the time.

"Some day man will fly," said Wilbur. "But it won't be in *our* lifetime — it won't be in a thousand years!"

## CHAPTER 9

# WILBUR GOES TO CHICAGO

Dayton, Ohio . . . the little frame house on Hawthorne Street . . . the bicycle shop. To these the brothers returned. To these they belonged. Henceforth, the mystery of flight they would leave to other men.

"We'll stick to what we can do," said Wilbur.

In time they might enlarge their bicycle business. In time the memory of Kitty Hawk would fade away.

So they thought. One person, however, thought otherwise. He was Octave Chanute. Aviation had no better friend than this wise, unselfish man.

Soon after the brothers reached home, Chanute wrote to them. He asked Wilbur to speak before the Western Society of Engineers, of which he was president.

Chanute had two reasons for his request. He believed Wilbur could give a welcome speech on a little-known subject; gliding. More important, he wished to keep alive the brothers' interest in flying.

He had seen these young bicycle makers in the air. He knew they were near to understanding the problems of flight, nearer than anyone in the world.

"Make a speech?" groaned Wilbur. "Never. I'd rather have lunch with a pack of lions."

"You can't refuse Mr. Chanute," said Orville. "He's gone to a lot of trouble to get you this chance."

"And you'll meet a lot of scientific men," said Katharine. "It will do you good, Will."

"I'll make an absolute jackass of myself," said Wilbur.

"Nonsense. You will not!" objected Katharine.

"I'll be standing before some of the best minds in the country," said Wilbur.

"You and Orv can teach anyone about flying!"

"You have to say that," said Wilbur. "You're my sister."

For an hour the protests went back and forth. Wilbur kept shaking his head and saying no. Orville and Katharine kept after him.

"Look," said Wilbur finally. "The meeting of the society is on the eighteenth. That's hardly two weeks away. I won't have time to prepare a full-length speech."

"Mr. Chanute will want you, even if you talk for only ten minutes," said Katharine.

Wilbur sighed. "You win — I'll write him. I'll tell him that a brief paper with pictures might interest a few members of the society. I'll make it sound terrible. He'll back down."

That night Wilbur sent off his letter. Four days later came Chanute's reply.

As Wilbur read it, his face paled.

"What does he say?" demanded Katharine. "Is it bad news?"

"Awful," said Wilbur. "He wants me to speak."

"What else does he say? Oh, Will, for heaven's sake! Stop acting like a scared little boy!"

"He asks what I shall call my speech," said Wilbur. "And listen to this: He would like to make the occasion Ladies Night!"

Wilbur sank weakly into a chair.

Katharine would have none of his play-acting. She brought him paper and pen. "Tell Mr. Chanute you'll be honored to speak."

"So long as my speech isn't the main part of the program," said Wilbur. He picked up the pen. " 'Late Gliding Experiments' strikes me as a good title."

As to the ladies, he wrote: "I will already be as badly scared as it is possible for a man to be, so that the presence of ladies will make little difference to me, provided I am not expected to appear in full dress."

For the next two weeks, he and Orville labored over the speech. On the day he was to leave, Katharine examined him from head to toe.

"You're not going like that!" she exclaimed. "Look at those trousers."

Wilbur looked thoughtfully at his baggy knees. He started for the kitchen to heat the flatiron.

"No, you don't," scolded Katharine. "You'll not press those old rags!"

"Take my clothes, Will," said Orville, who was more careful about his appearance.

Wilbur changed quickly. He boarded the Chicago train dressed in Orville's shirt, collar, cuffs, suit, and overcoat.

"I've got so much of Orv on me, I'm not sure which Wright brother will be speaking," he called through the train window.

He arrived in Chicago at 6:00 p.m., two hours before the meeting. Chanute was at the station. A half-hour later they were looking over lantern slides and the photographs Chanute had taken at Kitty Hawk.

Wilbur noted on the margins of his speech those pictures he would use. The hall was filling with men and women. He shook some hands and smiled.

"In two hours it will be over," he thought. "No matter what happens, in two hours the hall will be empty. I will be going home."

"It's eight o'clock," said Chanute.

Wilbur was aware of the sudden quiet. Dimly he heard Chanute's voice. Then Chanute had stopped talking and was bowing to him. There was polite applause.

Wilbur rose to his feet. The hand holding his speech was shaking; the papers rustled loudly. In horror, he imagined his mouth opening and no sound coming out.

He cleared his throat. "The difficulties," he began, "which stand in the path to success in flying are of three general classes. . . ."

His eyes moved steadily across the pages of his speech. On and on he talked. He did not have time to wonder how the speech was being received.

He told about the gliding done in 1900 and 1901 at Kitty Hawk. He gave credit to the work of others: Lilienthal, Pilcher, and Chanute. He declared his belief that powered flying was possible. He said nothing, however, of his own discouragement.

Almost before he knew it, he had arrived at the two main points of his speech. These were the problem of air tables and the question of models versus full-sized machines.

He spoke of Lilienthal's tables of air pressure against airplane surfaces, which everyone used. Boldly he declared that the tables might be seriously in error.

Wilbur was equally bold in the matter of gliding versus model building. He made it plain that he stood with the school of man-carrying gliders. He thought little of the school which believed in experiments with small, motor-driven models.

At length he came to the end. He gathered up his papers, bowed, and sat down. Above the pounding of his heart, he heard the applause. Chanute was beaming with delight.

In another few minutes the meeting was over. White-haired scientists left their seats to talk with the young birdman. Most of them were twice Wilbur's age. Some agreed with what he had said. Others did not. All treated him as their equal.

On the way to the railroad station, Chanute said, "Our journal comes out next month. You must send me a copy of your speech to publish."

"Here," said Wilbur. "You can have it right now. I won't need it any more."

Chanute held up his hand. "No. It is an important speech. Once in print, it will be read throughout the world. You may wish to make certain changes before it appears."

Wilbur did not quite understand what Chanute was driving at. Hadn't the speech been received handsomely? Wasn't it a success as it stood?

It needed Orville, back in Dayton, to explain.

"Chanute's faith in Lilienthal's air tables dies hard," said Orville. "He wants you to be sure you are correct before the speech is published."

"I did use some pretty strong words," agreed Wilbur.

"Perhaps I ought to soft-pedal that part of the speech."

"Then all we have to do is find out the truth," said Orville. "Prove we're right, and that Lilienthal and everyone else are wrong."

Suddenly Wilbur jumped to his feet. "If we're right, what does that mean?"

Orville looked up. "I don't know — what?"

"It means that other men had depended on wrong facts to conquer the air. It means that the reason they've all failed to fly *isn't because the thing can't be done.*"

Now Orville, too, was on his feet. They faced each other in high excitement. Wilbur started for the machine shop.

"We'll build a wind tunnel," he said eagerly. "Then we can take all kinds of measurements. We'll be able to control — "

He stopped in the middle of the sentence. He smiled at Orville.

"Octave Chanute," he murmured.

The grand old man had done more than get Wilbur to make a speech. He had got the Wright brothers to continue working on the problem of flight.

"Why, the old rascal," whispered Orville warmly.

CHAPTER **10**

# THE MAGIC BOX

IF THEY WERE going to fly, the brothers realized they had to go back to the beginning. To what supported a glider: to wind.

Just how did wind act upon wings?

And what was the best wing shape?

None of the known facts about the action of wind could be trusted. They had built two gliders using other men's figures. Both gliders had failed to lift as expected.

So the brothers cast aside the air tables they had used, and set out to learn the truth for themselves.

Being practical young men, they began in a practical way. They built a wind tunnel.

The tunnel was a wooden box, sixteen inches high, sixteen inches wide, six feet long. Air was blown into one end by a fan. (Since the bicycle shop lacked electricity, it was necessary to turn the fan by a homemade gasoline motor.)

To measure results, the brothers hooked up a system made of pieces of wire and hacksaw blades.

Next they built small models of two hundred different kinds of wings. Then the testing began. It was slow work. For more than two months they stood over the tunnel, trapping and studying the mystery of the wind.

They measured models of single wings, double wings, and triple wings, as well as wings set one behind the other. They measured "lift" and "drift." They measured thick surfaces and thin ones. They measured angles and curves. And they wrote down thousands of figures.

Gradually the tunnel led them closer to the truth. Each day another idea put forward by some famous man was found to be in error. Each day some number in a book was proved untrue.

The wooden box did not accept the words of famous men. It did not care what the books said. It could neither hear nor read. It was coldly honest. It knew two things only: wind, and the action of wind on different surfaces. It told the truth about both.

Slowly, a little bit each day, it gave up the secrets of flight.

With each new truth uncovered, the brothers grew more excited. They were like men sailing across new oceans, discovering new lands.

Never in all history had anyone put a wooden box

to such use. Late at night, while the world slept, Wilbur and Orville Wright were in their bicycle shop, testing, measuring, discovering.

Always, though, they were mindful of the cost. Flying could not yield them a living. They must soon begin work on next season's bicycles.

Shortly before Christmas they were forced to stop. They took the piles of figures and put them in order — into tables.

"Have a look," said Orville, when the last number had been set down.

Wilbur ran his hands over the sheets of paper. He enjoyed their feel. He did not have to look. He knew the wonder of those tables.

It was a moment of quiet victory. The old trial-and-error method was past. No longer would it be necessary to build flying machines one after another, hoping to get one that succeeded.

The neat, clean rows of figures ended guesswork. Men could now design, on paper, wings that would assure a successful flying machine.

But for Wilbur and Orville a new machine lay in the future. For the present, they turned their attention to bicycles.

Ten years earlier, the brothers had founded the Wright Cycle Company. Ten years they had struggled to build the business. They did not want to drop it for flying, in which they saw no money.

"I'm sorry we did not have time to carry some of our wind tests further," Wilbur wrote to Octave Chanute. "But having set a time for the tests to stop, we quit when the time was up.

"At least two thirds of my time in the past six months has been spent on the subject of flying," continued Wilbur. "Unless I decide to give myself to something other than a business career, I must pay closer attention to my regular work for a while."

Along with the letter, Wilbur sent Chanute copies of the wind-tunnel results.

"You have done a great work," Chanute wrote back, "and greatly advanced knowledge."

The older man regretted that the brothers had reached a stopping place. Yet he could not help but agree with them. He, too, saw no money in flying, except from possible exhibitions.

But he did see a way to get money to carry on the tests — a way he had voiced at their first meeting. He repeated it now.

He wrote: "If some rich man who wishes to connect his name with progress should give you ten thousand dollars a year to go on, would you accept? I happen to know such a man: Andrew Carnegie. Would you like me to write to him?"

The brothers were strongly tempted to say yes. What could be better than to give more time to flying? And to be well paid in the bargain!

They talked it over for several days. In doing so, they came face to face with a simple fact: they had become more interested in wings than in wheels.

Dared they give up the bicycle shop? Even if they succeeded in flying, what chance was there of ever making a good living at it? The Wright Cycle Company supported them quite well. In a few years it might even make them wealthy. In flying there was only the coin of hope.

"We can't quit the business," said Wilbur. "And if we stay in it, we have to give it most of our time. Then it wouldn't be fair to take outside money for part-time work in flying."

"It wouldn't be fair," agreed Orville. But he did not look at his brother.

A day passed. Still they put off answering Chanute. How they longed to take the ten thousand dollars, and stay in the bicycle business too! How easy it would be to fool some rich man — how very easy. Bicycle shop and flying machine — they could have them both. Who was to know? Who would use a stopwatch to see how they spent their time?

Two days before Christmas the brothers came to a decision. In his letter to Chanute, Wilbur made it sound simple: "I do not think it would be wise for me to accept help in carrying our present tests further."

It was not an easy decision. But like Wilbur and Orville Wright, it was honest. The brothers would go on alone.

During the winter they increased their bicycle business. When summer came, they had a comfortable amount saved. Not ten thousand dollars, but enough to allow for a few weeks away from the shop.

With the warm weather, their thoughts had returned to Kitty Hawk. They were eager to test their air tables. Moreover, they found themselves in a race for the clouds.

In all parts of the world men were attempting to fly. Prizes were to be offered by the great trade fair to be held in St. Louis. To the first man to fly would come both glory and money.

One man in particular had caught the world's fancy. He was Don Alberto Santos-Dumont, a wealthy Brazilian living in France. Overnight he had become famous.

"He went up in an airship," said Orville, reading a newspaper report. "Nobody seems to care whether you go up in a balloon or in a heavier-than-air craft. Just so long as you fly through the air."

"Don't take Santos-Dumont too lightly," warned Wilbur. "He's young and full of courage."

"So are a lot of other men," said Orville. "I suppose we ought to be thankful he's rich."

"Why?" asked Wilbur. "Is there some blessing in being poor?"

"No, but for Santos-Dumont being rich is a curse," said Orville. "He can afford mistakes too easily. He can build all the machines he wants to. He doesn't have to correct errors on paper first."

"You mean he doesn't have to bother with a wind tunnel," said Wilbur.

"I hope not," replied Orville.

To be the first to fly: suddenly that had become uppermost in the minds of Wilbur and Orville Wright.

Their wind tunnel had put them in the lead for the time being. It had given up a treasure more rare than jewels or gold. It had given up little hard truths. When put together, these truths would clear a path into the sky.

Aside from Chanute, the world did not know of their tunnel. Not yet. But the brothers feared that sooner or later others would construct boxes like theirs. Others would hear the wind speak its secrets.

That night Wilbur and Orville got out their air tables and began to build a new glider.

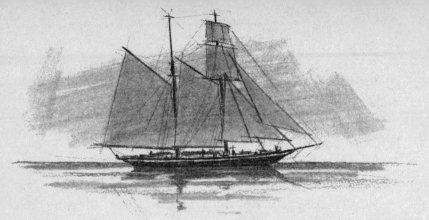

CHAPTER **11**

# CLOSER TO THE GOAL

**B**Y MIDSUMMER the bicycle rush was over. There was nothing to keep them in Dayton. So on August 25, 1902, the brothers set out for their third stay at Kitty Hawk.

The following evening they reached Elizabeth City. Here, less than a year before, Wilbur had given up hope.

"Some day man will fly," he had declared. "But it won't be in *our* lifetime — it won't be in a thousand years!"

The wind tunnel had changed everything. Out of the spin of a fan had come rows of numbers. Out of these numbers had come a new glider. And out of the glider was to come, the brothers believed, the means to fly.

Leaving Orville at the railroad station, Wilbur hurried to the waterfront. In a few minutes he returned.

"We're in luck," he reported. "There's a boat sailing

for Kitty Hawk at four tomorrow morning."

"We're going to need luck," said Orville. "It's six o'clock now. We haven't any food, and the stores will soon be closing."

"If we hurry, we can make it," said Wilbur. "It might be days before we can get another boat."

Even as he spoke, the gates of the baggage room closed. Inside were not only their trunks, but the boxes with the parts of the new glider. And they had been standing not ten feet away!

An old workman was turning the key in the lock. Both brothers shouted at once.

"Sorry, orders is orders. I got mine," said the old man. "Lock the gate at six at night, open it at six in the morning."

"But we can't wait till morning," said Orville. "We're in a terrible hurry."

"So it appears, young fella," was the answer. "Next time you're in such a terrible hurry, don't take the train. Just fly."

With that, the old man turned away, laughing at his little joke.

Orville took the chance. "We expect to do just that."

"What?"

"Fly."

The old man stopped. He looked the two young men over carefully. "You ain't the Wrights?"

"We are," said Wilbur.

"Well, I'll be darned," said the old man. He seemed suddenly like a small boy, filled with wonder. "I'll be darned," he said again, and opened the iron gate. "Go on, take your things."

Quickly the brothers carried out their boxes and trunks. "Many thanks," said Wilbur.

His thanks went beyond the workman's kindness. For the old man had done more than let them get their belongings. He had taught them how useful was fame.

In later years, fame opened doors all over the world for the Wright brothers. The iron gate was the first, and somehow it always remained the best.

After moving their boxes and trunks to the dock, the brothers rushed into town.

They bought a barrel of gasoline as the Standard Oil Company was closing. Orville got a tradesman to reopen his shop long enough to sell a small stove. Meanwhile, Wilbur found a grocery still doing business and bought several days' supply of canned goods.

It was an hour after dark before everything was loaded aboard the ship, the *Lou Willis*.

The brothers made themselves comfortable on deck and soon fell asleep. At three forty-five the next morning Captain Midgett awakened them.

"We're getting under way," he said.

He lifted anchor and put up sail. The schooner did not move. The sail hung empty. There was not a breath of wind.

"We'll have to use these," said the captain. He handed each brother a long pole. With the three men pushing along the bottom, the schooner moved slowly forward.

By six o'clock they had made a mile; by noon, six miles. Then the wind rose. Unfortunately, it came from dead ahead. Although the schooner picked up speed, it traveled mostly back and forth across the water. Kitty Hawk was very little nearer.

By three o'clock they had made about fifteen miles, or slightly less than a mile and a half an hour for eleven hours. When Captain Midgett saw he could not reach Kitty Hawk that night, he cast anchor.

The brothers lay down for their second night aboard ship. Each had his mind on their old enemy — wind.

Lack of wind caused the schooner to sit helplessly in the water. Lack of wind would cause their glider to sit helplessly on the sand.

"Are you thinking the same thing I'm thinking, Orv?" asked Wilbur.

"I guess so," said Orville.

The full moon cast a silver tail of light across the water and straight up to them. Little waves slapped gently against the ship.

"Man must be master of the wind, not its servant," said Wilbur. "Steamships move under their own power. So must gliders."

"Yes," said Orville. "But that's getting a bit ahead of ourselves."

"We're getting close," said Wilbur. "It doesn't do any harm to look ahead."

They lay side by side on the deck. Neither spoke in the stillness.

At last Wilbur said softly, "*A motor-driven flying machine!*"

Orville did not answer. He had rolled over and was fast asleep.

Late the next afternoon, the *Lou Willis* put in at Kitty Hawk. The brothers went at once to their old camp, Wilbur and the boxes by cart, Orville and the trunks in Bill Tate's small boat.

They found the wooden shed still standing, if knocked about. The ends had sunk two feet. The roof had a bump like a camel's back.

The shed had to be lifted and new posts put under the floor. Then the brothers built an addition, so as to have space for both the glider and living quarters.

It was fifteen days before the job of assembling the new machine was started. Working eight to ten hours a day, they made steady progress. If they were eager to get the glider done, they were also careful about getting it done right.

When they had finished the upper wings, they took it out for testing. The next day they finished the lower wings. Four days later the front rudder was done. Two more days saw the twin upright tails finished.

The tails were the biggest change over the earlier

gliders. But there were other changes. The wings, for example, were lengthened to thirty-two feet from tip to tip, ten more than the year before. In addition, control of the warping system was changed. The year before it had been worked by the feet. Now it was worked by the side-to-side movement of the hips, which rested in a "cradle."

On Friday, September 19, the glider was finally assembled. Orville took two pictures of her. Then she was carried from camp for her first trial.

As in the past, the brothers flew the new machine first as a kite. Three hours satisfied them. There would be no unpleasant surprises. They decided to try gliding.

"Which hill?" asked Dan Tate, Bill's brother, who had come to help.

The brothers looked toward the big Kill Devil Hill. On its steep sides they had made most of their glides the year before.

"Feel lucky?" Orville asked Wilbur.

"I sure do," said Wilbur. "We haven't been eaten by mosquitoes, and it hasn't rained too much."

"That isn't what I mean," said Orville. "Do you feel lucky enough to try the big hill?"

Wilbur stared at it. The big hill held the greatest thrills — and the greatest risks. "No," he said thoughtfully. "That one soon enough. Today we'll stick to a little one."

They glided on a little hill to the south. As usual, they

took great care. Not one glide was entirely free. Dan Tate and one of the brothers were always holding the wings.

The glides were short. Never did Wilbur or Orville take the machine up more than six feet. Mostly, they stayed within inches of the ground.

The machine handled well. In fact, it handled and acted the way their rows of numbers had said it would. They made about twenty-five glides.

These were simply feeling-out runs. The real trials were yet to come, on the big hill, in a strong wind. Yet the brothers had a hard time to keep from walking around with silly smiles on their faces.

Only one thing spoiled their joy. In the business of setting up camp, they had spent all their money. And they hated nothing worse than borrowing.

When they returned to camp, they found a letter from their sister Katharine. It ended the day on a perfect note.

Inside the letter was a badly needed twenty-five dollars.

CHAPTER **12**

# ALMOST PERFECT

During September, the new machine was tested both as a glider and a kite. Small changes were made every day. And every day the results were better.

The lack of lifting power, which had handicapped the two earlier gliders, was overcome. The controls worked just as expected. Those long, lonely hours at the wind tunnel were having their reward in the sky.

The brothers remained as careful and cautious as ever. But with each new success, they allowed their hopes to rise a little more.

One morning, Wilbur finished a glide and exclaimed, "She's almost perfect!"

She was exactly that — *almost.*

In making some fifty glides, the brothers had yet to meet with what was to happen this particular morning.

Wilbur was at the controls. He got the machine off nicely. In the first few seconds the glide looked very much like any of the others. Then everything looked different.

The machine turned sideways. She seemed to hang in the air. Then she came sliding to the ground. She struck on one wing and swung to a stop.

Wilbur got out, unhurt. "I gave the wings all the warp I could," he said. "It didn't help."

The brothers remembered something similar had happened the year before. Once in a great while the wing-warping system had failed to change the course of the machine. And for no reason that they could find.

"It isn't quite the same trouble as last year," said Wilbur. "I'm sure of that. This is something else."

"Why not try again?" said Orville. "The wind is holding steady. You'll have the same conditions."

The glider was carried to the top of the hill. Wilbur made three glides in a row. The machine handled beautifully.

"It wasn't the glider's fault. It was mine," he said. "I must have made some mistake. I'll bet it won't ever happen again."

But it did happen again. During the next week it happened three times. The glider would slide down through the air and dig a wing into the sand.

This occurred once when Wilbur was in the machine and twice when Orville was gliding. The wind hadn't changed. The controls moved properly. Nothing was different from the successful glides before and after.

Wilbur kicked at the deep hole which the wing had dug in the sand. "That's a hard way to dig a well," he commented angrily.

So did the mystery get a name — if nothing else. The brothers spoke of these accidents as "well-digging." How they wished they could blame themselves and not the machine!

Yet the fault was with the machine. So much was plain. Unless the trouble could be found and corrected, their high hopes were dashed. A flying machine could not be safe forty-nine out of fifty flights. It had to be safe *every* flight.

That evening they sat around the supper table with two guests and talked over the mystery. George Spratt, who had helped the year before, had come for a short visit. So had an older brother, Lorin Wright.

Spratt agreed that this new difficulty was not the same as the one last year.

"The machine seems to go into a kind of spin," he said. "That's something new."

"What changes have you made since last year?" asked Lorin.

"Too many," said Wilbur with a slight laugh.

"Well, what's the biggest change?"

"We added a tail," answered Orville.

Wilbur said, "The tail doesn't harm the machine. It improves it."

"Yes, but maybe you can improve the tail," said Lorin.

Wilbur leaned forward, smiling at his older brother. "It's like the nose on my face. Somebody else has to see it."

They talked over possible changes in the tail far into the night. They got nowhere.

Finally Wilbur rose yawning. "It's late, and I'm for bed."

The four men retired to their cots. Three dropped off to sleep quickly. One did not.

Orville had drunk too much coffee. Unable to sleep, he thought about the "well-digging" accidents — or tail spins as they were to be called in later years.

Never had too much coffee played so important a role in shaping the future. For as Orville lay, unable to sleep, he finally figured out what was wrong, and what to do about it.

The fixed tail had to be made into a *rudder that could be moved.*

At breakfast the next morning he told Wilbur.

"If we make the tail movable, we can shift the air pressure on it from the side toward the low wing to the side toward the high wing," he said. "In that way we can recover balance. Or make a turn toward the low wing."

He waited for Wilbur's answer. He expected his brother to say, "Oh, yes, I've already considered that. It won't work."

Instead, Wilbur sat quietly for a minute or two. Then he surprised Orville. Not only did he agree to Orville's reasoning, he went one step further.

"Why not hook up the rudder wires with those to the wing warping?" he suggested. "Then the pilot can work both at one time."

The brothers began to make the changes without delay. Two days later they had joined the two sets of wires. They also changed the design of the movable tail — from the double upright fins to a single rudder.

On the day the work was completed, their old friend Octave Chanute arrived in camp. He brought with him a helper, A. M. Herring, and a triple-decker glider of his own design.

As it was raining, no glides were possible. The next morning Herring took the Chanute glider out for a brief trial. After two more days of rain, the Chanute and Wright machines were tested together.

Herring attempted to glide first. He hung below the

triple wings in the old manner. He ran down the hill several times. But he could not get up enough speed. Panting and tired, he had to give it up.

Then the Wrights began. Wilbur lay down at the controls. He tried the wing warping and rear rudder, and the front rudder. He nodded to Orville.

With Orville and Spratt pushing, the big Wright glider took the wind almost instantly. It lifted and glided smoothly down the hill.

Wilbur did not try for distance. He was interested in the controls, not in showing off. But four short glides were enough to astonish Chanute and Herring.

Although disappointed in his own machine, Chanute was full of praise for the Wrights'. Before he left camp he saw Wilbur and Orville calmly perform feats that, three short years before, would have been considered impossible.

After their guests had all departed, the brothers really put their machine through her paces. During the last ten days at Kitty Hawk, they made more glides than in all the earlier weeks. In the last two days alone they made two hundred and fifty glides.

The brothers knew their serious troubles were over. The wind tunnel and the movable rudder had given them a machine other men dreamed about.

Now all that was needed was to gain skill by practice at the controls.

In gliding, they avoided risks. The high flights were

grand. But the low ones were fully as useful for training purposes. Quietly, on the lonely bar of sand, they were learning everything they wanted to know.

Some of their glides were more than six hundred feet. One lasted as long as twenty-six seconds. Many were made against winds of thirty-six miles an hour — a speed into which no one had ever before dared glide.

Watching the glider, Dan Tate said, "All she needs is a coat of feathers to make her light, and she'll stay in the air forever."

"She doesn't need feathers," said Orville. "She can beat the birds as she is."

It was a fact. The brothers had measured the angle at which hawks soar. They could glide at a smaller angle!

They had mastered balance. They had mastered wind. And they were mastering the machine. All that really remained was the last giant step — a motor.

At the end of October the brothers started home. Wilbur would have liked to practice longer. He wanted to be able to fly as naturally as he walked.

However, he hated to throw good money away. Their round-trip train tickets would run out on October 31. He saw no sense in buying new tickets when they might still use the old ones.

So flying was put away for the season. The brothers broke camp, and headed for Dayton and their bicycles.

CHAPTER **13**

# A NEW KIND OF ENGINE

T<small>HE</small> <small>ENGINE</small> the Wrights had in mind was something very special.

"It will have to be light, yet powerful," said Wilbur. "It must develop at least eight horsepower and weigh no more than two hundred pounds."

The brothers understood motors. They had built the one-cylinder engine which drove the wind-tunnel fan. Could they make the kind of engine they needed now?

After a few days' study, they decided against attempting so difficult a job. The wisest course was to buy an engine. But they found the engine they were seeking had not yet been made.

Wilbur wrote to a dozen automobile companies and engine manufacturers. He described exactly the engine he wanted. To lessen the weight, he suggested making the flywheel thinner and using more aluminum than usual. Could an order be delivered by May?

Eleven replies were received the following week. Each company said it was too busy to stop for one engine of such special design.

"That isn't their real reason for turning us down," said Orville. "They're afraid of what their regular customers will say. They don't want their names mixed up with anything as crazy as flying. It would hurt business."

The last reply arrived a week after the others. It was short and to the point. The company sold just the type of motors the Wrights needed. It developed eight horsepower, though weighing only one hundred and thirty-five pounds!

Wilbur immediately sent for more information. When it arrived, the brothers saw they had been misled. The motor had only one cylinder. It could not possibly be as powerful as was claimed.

"And that," said Wilbur heavily, "is that. We'll have to build our own motor after all."

They began the design at the end of December. By

stealing time from their bicycle business, they were able to complete a four-cylinder engine, weighing a hundred and fifty pounds, in less than two months.

The engine developed eleven horsepower, and up to sixteen at very high speeds. They had counted on eight only. The surprising power, plus the lightness of the engine, meant that the airplane could carry more weight than they had planned. The unused weight was promptly put into strengthening the wings and other parts.

On February 12, 1903, they ran their first tests. The following day an accident broke the engine body and frame. They had to send away for parts. Not until May could the rebuilt engine be tested.

In the meantime, they were anything but idle. They ran their bicycle business. They built gas radiators to heat their home. And they looked into the matter of propellers.

They had left propellers for the last. They had only to find out how water pressure acted on the screw propellers of powerboats. Then they could use their tables of air pressures instead of the tables of water pressures. Thus they could tell in advance what kind of air propeller would work best.

What could be more simple?

Full of confidence, the brothers went to the Dayton Public Library. They took out all the books they could find on the subject. They read — and got a surprise.

There were no tables of water pressures.

In fact, hardly anything was known about boat propellers.

The men who designed boats would try one propeller. If it did not push their boat fast enough, they would try a larger one, or one with a different angle.

No one could actually design a screw propeller and know beforehand what it would do in the water. Yet screw propellers had been in use for a hundred years!

"We can't just use any propeller and hope for the best," said Orville. "Once we're out at Kitty Hawk, it will be too late to make changes."

"And we don't have the time or money to test hundreds of propellers," said Wilbur.

The brothers had come to another dead end. It was the air-pressure tables all over again. Only this lack of knowledge about propellers was even more heart-breaking.

They had risked their lives at Kitty Hawk. They had built a machine that could ride on air. They had made an engine to power their machine. Had they done all this only to fail with success at their fingertips?

Propellers — an entirely new field to discover — lay before them, and there were no maps.

"We'll just have to find our way," said Wilbur. "We don't have much choice."

"The question is where do we begin? What do we measure first?" asked Orville. "The machine will be moving forward. The air will be rushing backward. The propeller will be turning sideways. Nothing will be standing in place."

It seemed an impossible task. But it was not the first impossible task the brothers had undertaken. They settled down to explore the propellers as they had explored the wind. Carefully. Step by step.

Month after month they kept at it. Slowly they tracked a way through the wilderness. By June, they had gained more knowledge of screw propellers than anyone had ever possessed. They felt certain they could design the propeller they needed.

Octave Chanute agreed with them. The Wrights' old friend stopped at Dayton after a five-month trip to Europe. He was excited by what the brothers had accomplished, and he told them about the interest their work had aroused in other parts of the world.

"The French are particularly taken with the idea of flight," he reported. "Many sportsmen are building heavier-than-air machines. Some of them have copied your 1902 model."

The brothers knew that Chanute had shown photographs of their glider in Europe. He had also praised their work in writing and in several speeches overseas.

Wilbur and Orville trusted Chanute. He did not mean to give out their secrets. He was a loyal friend. But the St. Louis Trade Fair was to be held next year, and two hundred thousand dollars in prizes would be offered to airmen.

Suppose somebody with a lot of time and money were to learn of their discoveries, beat them into the air, and win the contests in St. Louis!

Chanute's stories and speeches did not go deeply into the Wrights' discoveries. His words, however, had forced the brothers to face certain questions.

Should they give out all their discoveries, or only a few?

To give away everything would enable others to build machines that could fly. Lacking practice at the controls, these beginners would very likely injure or kill themselves.

To give out only a little information might result in quite as much danger. Men would hopefully build machines, thinking they had all the facts necessary. Instead of flying, they would crash.

The brothers had decided, even before Chanute's visit, to give out nothing. Now they made known their wishes to their friend.

"There is something else to consider," added Wilbur. "Last month we applied for patents in many countries. Germany and France will not allow a patent if any claims have been printed already."

"You're afraid that what I have written will be used against you? To deny you a patent on your machine?" asked Chanute.

"It might," answered Orville frankly.

"I am sorry," said Chanute. "I shall write no more of

what you are doing until you say I may."

Wilbur reddened. After all, Chanute had been like a father to them. Now the older man was leaning over backward not to hurt him or Orville.

"We don't mean to sound unthankful," said Wilbur. "Not after all your help —"

"Oh, I understand," Chanute assured them quickly. "You are perfectly right. You must do what you think best."

After an uncomfortable silence, Chanute started the talk going again. He spoke of other men's attempts to fly. The brothers listened, smiling inwardly.

For they had read the newspaper reports. Everywhere in the country airplanes were being built for the St. Louis Trade Fair. The builders had finished their machines, except for one or two small details, such as what size wing to use, or what kind of motor!

Then Chanute spoke of Professor Langley.

"He expects to test his new, full-sized power machine in October," said Chanute.

Langley would test in October! The news fell heavily upon the brothers. Langley was no daredevil, willing to risk his life for a thrill or glory. He was a serious student of flight — unlike most of the new crop of birdmen.

Now Langley was at the final stage, too. The race to conquer the air was rushing into the homestretch. And the world would be given the high drama of rivals no more alike than a prince and a plowman.

As head of the nation's Smithsonian Institution, Samuel Pierpont Langley was the leading scientist in America. The Wrights were almost unknown, and without training as scientists.

Further, the rivals belonged to opposite schools. Langley believed in building models. The Wrights believed in building gliders.

Now, after years of work, both were ready to test man-carrying machines.

Who would be the first to succeed?

By the end of the year 1903, history would have the answer.

CHAPTER **14**

# A TOSS OF THE COIN

THE LONG SHADOW of Samuel Pierpont Langley lay upon
the brothers all that summer of 1903. Langley's prepara-
tions were already well advanced when the Wrights
boarded a boat for Kitty Hawk.

"We're weeks behind him," said Orville, watching
the shore draw nearer and nearer.

The brothers could scarcely wait till they landed.
Wilbur sprang from the deck as the boat touched the
dock. He tripped and fell.

"This is getting foolish," he said, brushing himself off.

"We're both overanxious, Will," said Orville. "Let's forget Langley. We've got our own work to do. We won't get it done any faster with our minds on him."

When they reached camp, they discovered just how much work awaited them. The shed had blown two feet nearer the ocean, and in places was a foot lower. Repairs would cost them two days at least.

Moreover, they had decided to put up a second building. Then they could work on the new power machine indoors during rainy or windless days. On the days of good wind, they could practice with the 1902 glider. Surprisingly, she had suffered little harm during the winter.

They had arrived on Friday, and by Saturday they had started to work on the base of the new shed. In the beginning, everything seemed to favor them.

The work went without a hitch. The day was cool and clear. Even the hills of sand, which changed with the winds, were in the best shape ever.

On Sunday the brothers rested as usual. The weather on Monday continued to be so fine that they quit work after an hour. They took out the glider, adjusted her, and practiced gliding.

The results were amazing. They averaged better than 20 seconds a glide for 75 glides. A glide of Wilbur's lasted 30½ seconds, breaking their record.

Once Orville stayed up for 26 seconds while traveling

a mere 52 feet. The brothers considered this the great feat of the day. Orville had managed to float in one spot for 15 seconds — neither moving nor losing height.

This standstill flight was called hovering. Hovering was the best measure of a pilot's control of his machine, and the aim of every birdman.

The following Saturday the Wrights improved upon their records. Wilbur made a glide of 43 seconds in traveling 450 feet. This was about one eighth better than their record of the year before, and three times better than anyone else had ever done.

The brothers began to feel confident.

"With a little stronger wind, we ought to be able to stay up more than a minute," said Wilbur.

The kind of wind Wilbur wanted arose three weeks later. As a result, October 21, 1903, was the most remarkable day in gliding history.

The brothers made twenty glides. Wilbur remained in the air for more than a minute on four glides, and Orville on two. But the honors again belonged to Orville. He recorded the longest glide: one minute, eleven and four fifths seconds!

To any other birdman, such glides would have been the achievement of a lifetime. To the Wrights, the glides were simply proof that their system of balance was right.

They were not out to set records. Their purpose was to gain skill. And skill they were gaining. Every second added to their time in the air was the proof.

By now they had completed the new shed. And between hours on the sand hills, they worked inside. On November 5, they had the power machine assembled.

The power machine, like the gliders, had the appearance of a huge kite. She was bare of everything except what was needed to make her fly.

The wings spanned more than forty feet — eight feet longer than the big 1902 glider. The engine was set slightly to the right of center on the lower wing.

To balance the weight of the engine, the pilot would lie slightly to the left of center. The two propellers were placed outside the motor and pilot, and midway between the upper and lower wings.

The first test was limited to the engine. It took place inside the wooden shed. And ended quickly. Backfiring twisted one of the propeller shafts. There was a loud screech and wild thumping.

Wilbur leaped to shut off the motor. He was too late. The shafts tore loose and flew against the wall.

There was nothing to do now but ship the propeller shafts back to Dayton. Orville wrote to Charlie Taylor, their bicycle mechanic, telling him how to strengthen the shafts. Even if Charlie met no problems, it would be ten days before the new shafts reached Kitty Hawk.

George Spratt was in camp to witness the tests. The delay caused him to change his plans. He started home at once, taking the shafts as far as Norfolk, whence they would be shipped to Dayton.

Octave Chanute arrived the next day. As the weather was cold, and as there was no possibility of seeing a test flight, he stayed less than a week.

The new shafts, heavier and larger, reached the brothers on November 20. On the very first test, another difficulty appeared.

The sprockets which screwed into the propellers kept coming loose. It was a small problem. But the brothers did not know what to do about it.

They went to bed disappointed. Toward midnight, Orville rolled over, and called, "Will! Will — you remember that old stopwatch with the broken hands?"

"Sure. The watchmaker said it couldn't be repaired," replied Wilbur. "You fixed it right in the bicycle shop."

"With tire cement," said Orville. "I've got some in my trunk."

"Orv, you're a genius!" exclaimed Wilbur.

In the morning, they poured melted tire cement into the sprockets. As the cement had worked for their stopwatch, so it worked for their airplane. Loose sprockets were never again a problem.

The brothers looked forward to making a trial flight the next day. Again fate decided against them. The weather turned bad. Snow or rain fell for several days.

Though forced to remain indoors, they kept busy. They put together an automatic system for timing their flights. With it they could record the time from the moment the machine started forward until it landed, the distance traveled through the air, and the number of turns made by the motor and propellers.

On November 28, the brothers were satisfied that everything was in order. They were ready whenever the sky was. Just to be doubly sure, they ran several tests of the motor in the morning.

On the sixth test, they saw that something was wrong. They discovered one of the hollow propeller shafts had cracked.

Their hopes seemed to crack as well.

If they sent the propeller back to Dayton, they might not have it until January. Express service in the winter was slow and not to be trusted.

The days at Kitty Hawk were icy cold, the nights colder. The winds blew fiercely under rain-filled clouds. The brothers longed to be home for Christmas. Why not pack up and return in the spring? It would be easy to quit.

Wilbur stepped out of the shed. The water in the outdoor basin, he noticed, was frozen to the bottom. He beat his arms to keep warm.

A sea fog had rolled in. The sky was dark, though it was only a little past noon. A cold, gray loneliness pressed everywhere upon the land.

"It's cheerful enough inside," said Wilbur, coming into the shed again.

"The stove works fine," said Orville. "If we split up some logs, we could stay warm for a couple of weeks."

"Two weeks — that's long enough for one of us to take the shafts back to Dayton, isn't it?" observed Wilbur.

"I figured you would see it that way," said Orville.

Wilbur grinned. He took a coin out of his pocket. "Winner gets to ride on the train, sleep in a real bed, and eat Katharine's cooking."

Orville waited till the coin was in the air. "Heads!" he called.

Heads it was.

So Wilbur stayed on. He held that lonely spot of sand for Orville and himself. Wind and winter hurled themselves against him. But they could not wipe out the desire to fly.

Eleven days passed before Orville returned. Instead of hollow shafts, he brought shafts made of solid steel.

He also brought a two-day-old newspaper.

"Professor Langley has failed. He never got into the air."

Wilbur read the newspaper excitedly. Langley had attempted to fly from the top of a houseboat. The launching machinery had broken, and his airplane had immediately dropped into the Potomac River.

It was Langley's second attempt to fly his power machine, and his last.

Wilbur folded the paper. He said, "The machine never got a fair test. The newspapers make him appear a fool."

"All the newspapers are yelling with joy," said Orville.

"They are delighted Langley hasn't changed anything. What hasn't been done, can't be done!"

The brothers felt sorry for Langley. Yet his failure meant their only serious rival was out of the race.

Now there would be only birds to share the sky with them.

CHAPTER  **15**

# ON THE TRACK

Six days after Professor Langley's downfall, the Wrights finally had their own machine ready.

They planned to fly her on Monday, December 14. The day dawned cold and clear, but the wind blew at only five miles an hour.

"That's not enough to allow a start from level ground," said Orville.

"We can get a good start from Kill Devil Hill," replied Wilbur. "Up there the lack of wind will actually help us. The machine will be far easier to handle."

"Then let's try the hill," said Orville. "I'll put up the signal."

He went out and hung a sheet from the wall of the shed. It meant a trial of the power machine would be made that day.

The brothers were eager for witnesses. Yet it was impossible to go about knocking on doors without wasting hours. So the sheet had been decided on as a general invitation to all.

Soon six big men from the Kill Devil Lifesaving Station came into camp.

"The machine weighs seven hundred and fifty pounds," Wilbur told them. "We'll need your help in moving her to the hill."

In no time the lifeguards had the machine out of the shed.

"Which hill?" they wanted to know.

"The big hill," answered Wilbur. "You can set her down right where you are. We'll roll her the rest of the way."

"Roll her?" asked one of the men. "How? She has no wheels."

"Oh, it can be done," said Orville.

The brothers carried out four pieces of wooden two-by-fours. Each piece was fifteen feet long and covered by metal. Put together, the four pieces formed a sixty-foot rail.

"This is our starting track," explained Wilbur. "We'll use it for taking off."

Orville set a little truck on the rail. He said, "Now,

gentlemen, if you'll lift the machine onto the truck, we can get moving."

"The rail is only sixty feet long," objected a lifeguard. "The hill is a quarter-mile away. I still don't see how you can roll her there."

"Very simple," said Wilbur. "Lend a hand."

The machine was placed atop the little truck. With the men pushing, truck and flying machine moved smoothly over the rail.

As the first piece of rail was passed over, Wilbur and Orville picked it up. Quickly they carried it forward and laid it at the front end.

The lifeguards caught on, with a laugh.

"Once you know the answer, a puzzle looks real simple," said one.

Thereafter the lifeguards undertook the job of picking up the back rail and moving it to the front. By doing this over and over, they reached the foot of the hill.

The rail was then laid on the slope, a hundred and fifty feet up. The machine was run to the top of the rail and roped into place. Both brothers were now excited. Both wanted to make the first flight.

"Let's flip a coin," suggested Orville. "Here," he said, fishing in his pocket. He brought out a nickel. "You call it."

Wilbur watched the nickel spin off Orville's thumb and rise high in the air. It landed in the sand with a soft *plop* a second after Wilbur had cried, "Tails!"

The brothers bent over the coin. Orville had to brush away the sand with a finger before they could see it.

"You win, Will."

Wilbur hurried to the machine. In a moment he had the motor roaring loudly.

Two small boys and their dog had come over to watch. When the motor roared, they took to their heels in fright.

"It's all right," Orville cried after them. "It won't hurt you."

The lifeguards called, too. But nothing could bring the boys back. The strange thing on the hill looked like a giant bird and made noises like a hundred lions.

Wilbur let the motor run for several minutes. When he was satisfied that it was working properly, he lay down in the cradle.

Orville stood by the right side, ready to help balance the machine as it moved down the rail. In his free hand he held a stopwatch.

Wilbur began to untie the rope which held the machine. Looking down the hill, he saw the rail had not been laid exactly straight. That would make the start difficult.

He noticed, too, that the wind had shifted, coming a little from the side.

A terrible doubt flashed through his mind. He was lying in a machine that had never been tested as a kite or glider. On paper, it was fine — and safe. All their years of work and study said this machine would fly — fly five miles, if everything went as it should.

Yet what if something had been overlooked?

Something was already going wrong. The holding rope would not come loose.

"Give me a hand," Wilbur shouted.

Two lifeguards ran over. At his bidding they pushed the machine farther uphill. The rope slipped loose.

Suddenly the machine was in motion. Orville was still waving to the man at the other side to let go. He had to grab hastily onto an upright wing post.

Off went the two brothers — one in the machine, the other running to keep up.

Orville stayed even for about thirty-five feet. Then he was forced to let go. The machine raced free. Six feet from the end of the rail, Wilbur lifted her into the air.

With the motor thundering, the machine rose to fifteen feet. After traveling sixty feet, the front end went up suddenly. The forward speed slowed, and the machine began to lose altitude.

Wilbur tried to correct the error. As the machine was coming down, he succeeded in picking up a little speed. Too late. The machine continued to sink while still turned up in front.

The left wing dipped low and hit first. The machine spun around and dug through the sand to a stop. It was several seconds before Wilbur remembered to shut off the engine.

The entire flight had lasted three and a half seconds.

The distance traveled was a hundred and five feet.

For this poor showing Wilbur blamed himself.

"I turned up too soon after leaving the rail," he said. "She hadn't enough speed yet to support any move like that. If I had waited another few seconds, the flight might have been what we expected."

Despite the brief time in the air, the brothers were not altogether disappointed.

The controls worked fine. The machine was strong — only a few sticks in the front rudder were broken. And the method of launching had proved itself.

"I had no trouble staying on the track," said Wilbur. "We won't have the same difficulty that broke Professor Langley's heart. We can get our machine into the air."

The brothers regarded the three-and-a-half-second flight as a false start. Still to be answered was the big question: Could the machine fly under its own power?

Before they could find out, they had to repair the broken rudder. The job was completed the evening of December 16.

That night they lay awake listening to the wind. It blew fiercely, chilling the inside of the building. Between the cold and their own excitement, neither Wilbur nor Orville got much rest.

In the morning, the wind was still blowing fiercely. The brothers walked outside to have a look at the ground. Pools of water from the recent rains had frozen into ice. The wind made the brothers' cheeks burn.

Wilbur took a reading. "It's blowing at twenty-seven miles an hour," he said.

"We'd better wait," said Orville. "By ten o'clock it might die down."

The brothers retired to the warmth of their stove. An hour passed, then two, then three. The wind blew as strongly as ever.

At ten o'clock Orville said, "It's not going to die down."

"No," said Wilbur. "It's not. Are you game?"

By way of answering, Orville rose and went outside. He returned in less than a minute.

That was all it took him to hang out the signal for the people of Kitty Hawk.

The wind tore at the sheet but could not rip it down. Its message carried across the miles of white beach.

The Wright brothers were going to fly today.

CHAPTER **16**

# BIRTH OF THE SPACE AGE

W HAT DOES it measure now?" asked Orville.

Wilbur glanced at his hand anemometer. "The same — still twenty-seven miles an hour."

"Why, that's excellent," Orville sang out. "A strong wind will slow the landing speed."

Wilbur nodded wisely. "What could be safer than flying in a storm?"

"Flying in good weather, perhaps," said Orville.

"Oh, anybody can fly then," replied Wilbur lightly.

Although they joked, the brothers knew the danger.

The wind was an old foe. They had learned its tricks from their tunnel, their study of propellers, and their three years of gliding.

But now they faced a wind stronger than they, or any birdman had ever faced.

An added concern was the biting cold. Frequently the brothers had to stop work and warm up by the stove. Despite these breaks, they managed to lay the starting rail. Their airfield was a level stretch of ground a hundred feet west of camp.

As they were finishing, company arrived. The signal sheet had been seen. Into camp came three members of the lifesaving crew, a man from Manteo, and a boy from Nag's Head.

Wilbur and Orville were disappointed that Bill Tate was not among the party.

"I guess he figures nobody but a crazy man would try to fly in this wind," said Orville.

With the help of the lifeguards, the brothers set the machine upon the little truck. It was Orville's chance at the controls. Wilbur had used up his turn three days before in the 3½-second flight which the brothers still considered not a true flight but a false start.

Orville started for the machine. Suddenly he stopped and walked into one of the buildings.

"We forgot this," he said, bringing out a camera. "A picture might be useful."

Orville set the camera on a stand between the buildings and the machine. He aimed it so that the end of the rail was in the center of its five-by-seven-inch glass plate. John T. Daniels, a lifeguard, was given the job of snapping the picture.

With everything in readiness, the brothers heated up the motor. Orville lay down in the cradle.

Like Wilbur, he wore a high starched collar and necktie. He looked more like a bank clerk than a man about to attempt a miracle.

It was 10:35 a.m., Thursday, December 17, 1903.

All over the world, men and women were going about their daily business. Horse-drawn carts and bicycles traveled the roads. Boats sailed the waters. A streetcar fire made the front page of the *New York Times*.

And unnoticed on the sands of tiny Kitty Hawk, a piece of machinery waited to lift itself off the earth and fly.

Orville undid the holding rope. Slowly the machine moved forward into the wind.

Too slowly, Orville thought. "Come on," he urged.

Out of the corner of his eye he saw Wilbur. His brother was running alongside. He was having no trouble in staying even.

"The wind," Orville thought. "It's too strong. I can't get up enough speed!"

The machine traveled down the rail . . . twenty feet . . . twenty-five . . . thirty . . . thirty-five . . .

"Faster," Orville pleaded "Faster!"

Twenty feet to go to the end of the raill Then a spill into the sand —

Fifteen feet to go . . . ten . . .

All at once the machine gave a little bounce. Orville knew he was off the truck. He passed over the end of the rail, two feet above the ground.

With every second the machine gathered speed. The motor roared. The wings shook. Orville's eyes teared from the sting of the wind. Eager to get more height, he worked the rudder. The airplane rose to ten feet — and darted for the ground.

Orville got the front up. After going another thirty feet, the machine again darted down. This time Orville was too slow. Before the front could be lifted, the runners had struck the sand.

The flight had covered a hundred and twenty feet. It had lasted twelve seconds. A flight shorter than a city block and lasting less time than the flame of a match.

Yet what Orville had done fulfilled the dream of mankind. He had *flown*.

For the first time, a machine had raised itself off the ground by its own power. It had traveled through the air without losing speed. And it had come to earth at a point as high as the spot from which it had taken off.

This was not a chance flight. The brothers were to make three more, each better than the first.

After warming up beside the stove, Wilbur took the controls at 11:20 a.m. The wind had let up slightly. He

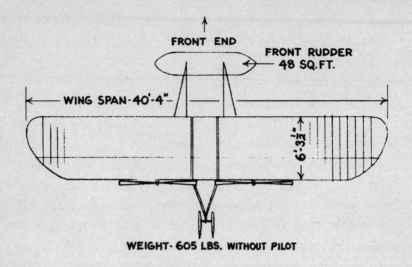

↑
FRONT END

FRONT RUDDER — 48 SQ.FT.

|← WING SPAN·40'·4" →|

6'·3½"

WEIGHT· 605 LBS. WITHOUT PILOT

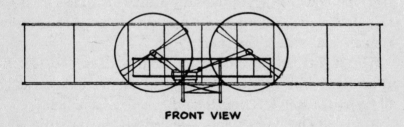

FRONT VIEW

was able to fly faster than Orville, and 75 feet farther.

Twenty minutes later Orville made his second flight. He flew more steadily than on his first attempt. He kept the machine up 15 seconds and went 200 feet.

Wilbur made the fourth and last flight at noon. As in the earlier flights, the beginning seconds were full of rough ups and downs.

After flying 300 feet, Wilbur had the machine under

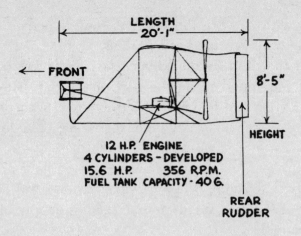

LENGTH
20'-1"

← FRONT

8'-5"

HEIGHT

12 H.P. ENGINE
4 CYLINDERS – DEVELOPED
15.6 H.P.      356 R.P.M.
FUEL TANK CAPACITY · 40 G.

REAR
RUDDER

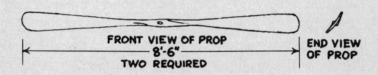

FRONT VIEW OF PROP
8'-6"
TWO REQUIRED

END VIEW
OF PROP

better control. Then for an amazing 500 feet, he flew evenly.

The flight ended in one of the machine's familiar downward darts. The front rudder hit the ground hard and broke.

"The rest of her seems okay," said Wilbur, checking the frame quickly. "We ought to have her fit again tomorrow."

Fired with success, the brothers now hoped to continue the trials for another few days.

When the distance of Wilbur's last flight was measured, it was found to be the best of the day. He had flown 852 feet and had stayed in the air 59 seconds.

Not for years would any other flier come close to this record!

The broken rudder was removed, and the machine carried back to camp. Wilbur put the camera away while the rest of the men stood around, talking quietly of the day's triumphs.

Suddenly a gust of wind caught the machine. All raced to hold down the wings. Orville and John Daniels seized the uprights at the rear.

The wind was too strong for them. Orville shouted, "Let go!" as the machine began to turn over.

John Daniels had mistakenly taken hold of the inside, for he knew little about flying machines. He was thrown over and over, trapped in with the engine and chains.

There was no way to help him till the wind passed. Head over heels he went till the machine stopped.

He got out painfully. "That was a close one," he said. He ran his hands over his sides, feeling for broken bones. "Seems like I'm all right."

"Are you sure?" asked Wilbur.

John Daniels nodded, and grinned. "If that thing is as hard to control in the air as on the ground, you fellows must be pretty good."

Once they were certain John Daniels was unharmed, the brothers gave their attention to the machine. The engine legs had snapped off, the chain guides were bent, and several uprights were smashed.

"That does it for the year," said Orville sadly.

Wilbur, too, saw there was no chance of flying again. The machine was ruined.

The brothers carried the wreck inside the shed. After eating lunch, they set out for the government weather bureau station to send a telegram to their father. It was past three o'clock when they arrived.

Orville had written out the message on a piece of brown paper. As he read it over, he decided to make a change.

"I wrote that we flew against a twenty-seven-mile-an-hour wind," he said. "That makes the flights sound harder than they were."

"The wind was a lot less on two flights," agreed Wilbur.

Rather than take a fraction more credit than was their due, Orville underplayed the speed of the wind. His corrected message read:

SUCCESS FOUR FLIGHTS THURSDAY MORNING ALL AGAINST 21-MILE WIND STOP  STARTED FROM LEVEL WITH ENGINE POWER ALONE STOP  AVERAGE SPEED THROUGH AIR 31 MILES LONGEST 59 SECONDS STOP INFORM PRESS STOP HOME CHRISTMAS.

ORVILLE

After leaving the weather bureau building, the

brothers walked over to the lifesaving station to chat with some of the men.

They walked slowly across the sand. Above them the afternoon sun shone brightly. The endless sky was clear and blue.

The brothers did not look up. They knew that the sky was without a cloud and that it was blue.

They had been there.